CHINESE
COOKERY

CHINESE COOKERY

Deh-ta Hsiung

CONTENTS

INTRODUCTION
PAGE 6

COLD STARTERS & BUFFET DISHES
PAGE 14

SOUPS
PAGE 28

QUICK STIR-FRIED DISHES
PAGE 34

BRAISED & STEAMED DISHES
PAGE 54

RICE, NOODLES & PANCAKES
PAGE 72

INDEX
PAGE 80

First published in 1983 by Octopus Books Limited
59 Grosvenor Street, London W1

© 1983 Hennerwood Publications Limited

ISBN 0 86273 0651

Produced by Mandarin
Publishers Ltd
22a Westlands Road
Quarry Bay
Hong Kong

Printed in Hong Kong

INTRODUCTION

It has been established that trade and cultural exchanges between China and the outside world took place as early as the time of the Roman Empire and for centuries many aspects of Chinese civilization were admired in the West and influenced its cultural development; yet Chinese culinary art, one of China's greatest heritages, was comparatively unknown in the West until recent times.

If you have always wanted to try cooking Chinese food but have been put off by the daunting thought of exotic ingredients and complicated techniques, my advice is to forget those unfounded fears. As you will soon discover, basic Chinese cooking is really quite simple. In this book there is a variety of recipes mostly from my own home cooking representing a wide range of China's various regional styles. I have also included a number of dishes that could be termed specialities but nothing very elaborate or time-consuming.

Due to the multi-course nature of a Chinese meal, menu-making requires much more thought and consideration than the planning of a Western menu. The recipes in this book are arranged so as to simplify the process.

Since not all Chinese ingredients are obtainable in this country, adequate substitutes are suggested, where they do not spoil the genuine Chinese flavour. What you must remember is that a Chinese cook abroad can always produce a Chinese meal, even using only local ingredients. For the 'Chineseness' of the foods depends entirely on *how* it is prepared and cmokef, not *what* ingredients are used.

The main characteristics of Chinese cooking

The main distinctive feature in Chinese cooking is the harmonious balance of colours, aromas, flavours and form in one single dish.

色 **Colour** (se): Each ingredient has its own colour, certain items change their colour after cooking. The cook should bear this in mind when selecting different ingredients for blending of colours.

香 **Aroma** (xiang): Again each ingredient has its own aroma or fragrance, some sharp, some subtle. Most meats and fish have a rather strong smell and need a strong agent both to supress this and to enhance their real aroma when cooked. Chinese rice wine is used in cooking for this purpose (dry sherry is a good substitute). Other much used seasonings are spring onions, ginger root and garlic.

味 **Flavour** (wei): Flavours or tastes are closely related to aromas and colours and the principle of blending complementary flavours is a fundamental one – the different ingredients must not be mixed indiscriminately; the matching of flavours follows a set pattern and is controlled, not casual.

形 **Form** (xing): The cutting of ingredients is important in achieving the proper effect. Slices are matched with slices, shreds with shreds, cubes with cubes and so on. This is not just for the sake of appearance, which is an important element of Chinese culinary art but also because ingredients of the same size and shape require about the same amount of time for cooking.

This complexity of interrelated elements of colour, aroma, flavour and form in Chinese cooking is reinforced by yet another feature: texture. A dish may have just one or several textures, such as tenderness, crispiness, crunchiness, smoothness and softness. The textures to be avoided are: sogginess, stringiness and hardness. The selection of different textures in one single dish is an integral part of the blending of flavours and colours.

Regional cooking styles

The fundamental character of Chinese cooking remains the same throughout the land: from the Peking cuisine in the north to the Cantonese cooking in the south, all food is prepared and cooked in accordance with the same principle: that most ingredients are cut up before cooking, with great emphasis laid on heat control and the harmonious blending of different flavours. However, what distinguishes one region from the other is that in the north, people eat more wheat-flour food as their bulk, whilst it is almost always rice in the south. Some of the cooking methods may vary a little from region to region; also the emphasis on seasonings may differ, but basically they are all unmistakably "Chinese".

Traditionally, the various styles of cooking are classified into four major groups according to their localities.

The Eastern Region is represented by China's largest city, Shanghai, with a population of well over 12 million. The cuisine of Shanghai is strongly influenced by the regional styles from the Yangtse River delta, particularly by the sophisticated school known as Huaiyang. The characteristics of this region can be best summarized as exquisite in appearance, rich in flavour and sweet in taste.

The Southern Region is represented by China's most diverse school of cuisine from Canton in the Pearl River delta. Because Canton was the first Chinese port opened for trade, foreign influences are particularly strong in its cooking. Together with the neighbouring province of Fujian (Fukien), Canton is the place of origin of many Chinese emigrants overseas, therefore this is also the best known style of Chinese cooking abroad.

The Western Region is represented by the richly flavoured and piquant food of Sichuan. The use of hot chilli in cooking is not supposed to paralyse your taste buds, but rather to stimulate your palate. The neighbouring province of Hunan is also renowned for hot, peppery cooking but has, in addition, a distinctive style of its own.

The Northern Region is represented by Peking, China's capital for many centuries. Because it is the political and cultural centre of China, Peking has accumulated the best cooking styles from all the other regional schools, thereby becoming China's culinary centre as well as creating a cuisine of its own.

You will find recipes from all these regional styles of cooking in this book. A few of these I have slightly adapted for practical reasons, but the majority I have left unaltered in order to preserve their authenticity.

Basic techniques of cooking methods

Slicing: This is probably the most common form of cutting in Chinese cooking. The ingredients are cut into very thin slices not much bigger than a large postage stamp, and as thin as cardboard.

Shredding: The ingredients are first cut into thin slices, then stacked up like a pack of playing cards and cut into thin strips about the size of matchsticks.

Dicing: The ingredients are first cut into coarse strips about the size of potato chips, then diced into cubes about the size of sugar lumps.

Diagonal cutting: This method is normally used for cutting vegetables such as carrots, celery, courgettes or asparagus. Roll the vegetable half a turn each time you make a vertical diagonal cut.

Mincing or finely chopping: The ingredients are finely chopped into small bits. Although it is much easier and quicker to use an electric mincer, the flavour and texture are not quite the same.

Flower-cutting: Kidneys, squid and tripe are usually cut in this manner. First score the surface of each piece diagonally in a criss-cross pattern, then cut the ingredients into small pieces so that when cooked, each piece will open up and resemble ears of corn, hence the name 'flower'.

A map of the four main regional cuisines of China

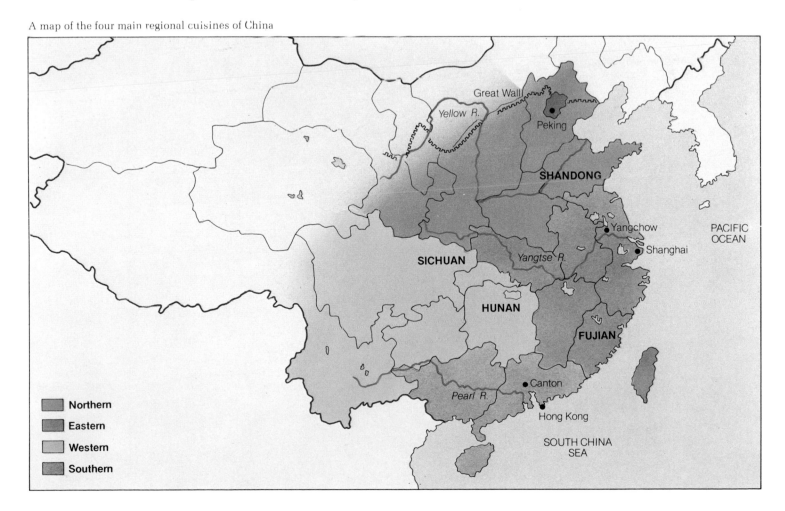

Northern
Eastern
Western
Southern

Great Wall
Yellow R.
Peking
SHANDONG
Yangchow
Shanghai
PACIFIC OCEAN
SICHUAN
Yangtse R.
HUNAN
FUJIAN
Canton
Pearl R.
Hong Kong
SOUTH CHINA SEA

Chopping: The normal method of cutting a whole cooked chicken or duck across the bones is as follows:

1. Remove the two wings, the legs and thighs.

2. Separate the breasts from the backbone.

3. Cut the backbone into about 8 pieces, place them on the bottom of a serving dish. Cut each wing into 2-3 pieces, place them on each side of the backbone.

4. Cut each leg and thigh into 3-4 pieces, place them on the edge of the plate.

5. Split the breasts down the middle, then cut each breast into 3-4 pieces. Reassemble them on top of the backbone as neatly as possible.

After cutting, the next step in the preparation of food before actual cooking is marinating. The basic method is to marinate the fish or chicken in salt, egg white and cornflour, in order to preserve the natural delicate texture of the foods when cooked in hot oil. For meat the basic marinade is salt, sugar, soy sauce, rice wine and cornflour and sometimes oil is added. The purpose of this marinating is to enhance the flavours of the meat. After egg whites have been used in a marinade, the left-over yolks can be used in cake-making or added to the egg mixture in recipes using scrambled eggs or omelettes.

The desired texture or textures in any dish can only be achieved by the right cooking method. The various cooking methods can be grouped under four basic categories: water-cooking, oil-cooking, steam-cooking and fire-cooking.

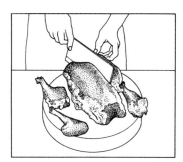

Removing the legs and thighs after the wings.

Separating the breast from the backbone.

Cutting each wing into 2-3 pieces.

Splitting the breasts down the middle.

TOP TO BOTTOM: Cellophane noodles; Bamboo shoots; Light soy sauce; Bean sprouts; Soaked and dry wooden ears; Chilli bean paste; Egg noodles

Water-cooking:

汆 Chuan – Rapid boiling over a high heat. Thinly sliced or shredded ingredients are dropped into boiling stock or water to be cooked for 1-2 minutes only. Most soup dishes are cooked in this way.

煮 Zhu – Boiling over medium heat under cover. This is used for dishes requiring long cooking, such as *Salted peking duck* (page 20) and the casserole dishes.

炖 Dun – Simmering over a low heat under cover. Dishes such as *Crystal-boiled pork* (page 22) or *'Lion's head'* (page 63) are cooked by this method.

炝 Qiang – Blanching in boiling water, then dressing with sauce, see *Peking poached prawns* (page 14).

Oil-cooking:

炒 Chao – Stir-frying over a high heat. Thinly sliced or shredded ingredients are stir-fried in a little hot oil for a very short time.

爆 Bao – Rapid-frying over extreme heat. *Bao* literally means to explode. See *Rapid-fried prawns in shells* (page 14) or *Rapid-fried lamb slices* (page 42).

炸 Zha – Deep frying over a medium heat.

煎 Jian – Shallow frying over a medium heat.

烧 Shao – Stewing over a low heat, such as *Spiced beef* (page 22).

滷 Lu – Soy-braising, such as *Braised tripe* (page 20).

烩 Hui – Another form of braising. *Hui* literally means 'assembly'. Normally a number of ingredients, some cooked, some semi-cooked, are blended together for the final stage of cooking in gravy. See *Chicken wings assembly* (page 57).

Steam-cooking:

蒸 Zheng – Steaming. In Chinese cooking there are two methods of steaming: firstly, a plate or bowl containing the ingredients is placed on the bottom rack of a steamer, which is then put inside a wok containing boiling water, so that the steam passing through the steamer cooks the food. The second method is to place the plate or bowl containing the ingredients on a wire or bamboo rack which fits half way down in a wok containing boiling water. Cover the wok and the food is cooked by the rising steam inside the wok. The traditional English aluminium steamer can be used for the smaller dishes.

Fire-cooking:

烤 Kao – Roasting in an oven.

叉 烧 Cha Shao – Barbecuing on an open fire.

Special ingredients and seasonings

As I said earlier, a Chinese cook does not need special ingredients in order to produce a Chinese meal. However, there are certain items which are commonly available in this country which will add just that exotic touch to your everyday cooking.

Bamboo shoots: Available in cans only. Once opened, the contents may be kept in fresh water in a covered jar for up to a week in the refrigerator. Try to find *Winter bamboo shoots* which are extra tender and delicious.

Bean curd: Also known as *To fu*, this custard-like preparation of puréed and pressed soya beans is exceptionally high in protein and is known in China as the 'poor man's meat'. It is sold in cakes about 7½ cm (3 inch) square and 2½ cm (1 inch) thick in Oriental and health food stores. Will keep for a few days if submerged in water in a container and placed in the refrigerator.

Bean sprouts: Fresh bean sprouts, from mung beans, are widely available from most supermarkets. They can be kept in the refrigerator for two to three days. Canned bean sprouts should not be used as they do not have the crunchy texture which is the main characteristic of this popular vegetable.

Cellophane or transparent noodles: Made from mung beans, they are sold in dried bundles weighing from 50 g (2 oz) to 450 g (1 lb). Soak in warm water for 5 minutes before use.

Chilli bean paste: Fermented bean paste mixed with salt, flour and hot chilli. It is sold in jars. Chilli sauce mixed with crushed *Yellow bean sauce* is a substitute. The amount of chilli sauce used depends entirely on personal taste.

Chilli sauce: Hot, red sauce made from chillis, vinegar, sugar and salt. Use sparingly in cooking or as a dip sauce. Tabasco sauce can be substituted.

Chinese dried mushrooms (*Lentinus edodes*): Widely used in many dishes as a complementary vegetable both for their flavour and aroma. Soak them in warm water for 20-30 minutes (or in cold water for several hours), squeeze dry and discard the hard stalks before use. Continental dried mushrooms, though of slightly different flavour and fragrance, can be substituted.

Cooking oil: In China, the most popular cooking oil is made from peanuts, followed by soya beans, rape seeds or other seeds such as sunflower or cotton. Lard and chicken fat are sometimes used but never butter or dripping.

Dried shrimps: They come in different sizes and have been salted and dried in the sun, they should be soaked in warm water for at least 30 minutes, then drained and rinsed before use. They will keep in the dry state in an air-tight container indefinitely.

Five-spice powder: A mixture of star anise, fennel seeds, cloves, cinnamon and Sichuan pepper, it is very strongly piquant, so should be used sparingly. It will keep in a tightly covered container for years.

Ginger root: Sold by weight, should be peeled and sliced or finely chopped before use. It will keep for weeks in a dry, cool place. Ginger powder is no substitute.

Hoi Sin sauce (also known as barbecue sauce): Made from soy bean sauce, sugar, flour, vinegar, salt, garlic, chilli and sesame seed oil. Will keep in the refrigerator for several months.

Oyster sauce: A thickish brown sauce made from oysters and soy sauce. Sold in bottles, it will keep in the refrigerator for several months.

Prawns: In Britain, small prawns are usually sold cooked either in their shells or peeled. The larger variety known as Pacific or king prawns, frozen when fresh, are sold uncooked, always in their shells. They should be thoroughly defrozen before cooking.

Red bean paste: This reddish-brown paste is made from puréed red beans and crystallized sugar. It is sold in cans. Once opened, the contents should be transferred to a covered container and will keep in the refrigerator for several months. Sweetened chestnut purée can be substituted.

Rice wine: Also known as Shaoxing wine, made from glutinous rice. *Sake* or pale (medium or dry) sherry can be substituted.

Salted black beans: Very salty indeed! Sold in plastic bags, jars or cans. Should be crushed with water or rice wine before use. Will keep indefinitely in a covered jar.

Sesame paste: Sold in jars covered with oil and resembles clay in colour and consistency but is extremely aromatic, rich and tasty. Stir well to make it into a creamy paste before use. Peanut butter creamed with sesame seed oil is a possible substitute.

Sesame seed oil: Sold in bottles and widely used in China as a garnish rather than for cooking. The refined yellow sesame oil sold in Middle Eastern stores is not so aromatic, has less flavour and therefore is not a very satisfactory substitute.

Sichuan peppercorns: Also known as *hua chiao*, this reddish-brown peppercorn is much stronger and more fragrant than either black or white peppercorns. Sold in plastic bags, will keep for a long time in a tightly sealed container.

Sichuan preserved vegetable: This is a speciality of Sichuan. It is the root of a special variety of the mustard green pickled in salt and chilli. It is sold in cans. Once opened, the contents should be transferred to a tightly covered container and will keep for months in the refrigerator.

Soy sauce: Sold in bottles or cans, this most popular Chinese sauce is used both for cooking and at the table. Whenever possible, and unless stated in the recipe, use *Light soy sauce* which has more flavour and does not discolour the food as much as the *Dark soy sauce*.

Water chestnuts: Available both fresh or in cans. Canned water chestnuts are peeled and will keep in fresh water for several weeks in a covered jar in the refrigerator.

Wooden ears: Also known as *Cloud ears*, they are dried black fungus (*Auricularia auricula*). They should be soaked in water for 20 minutes, then rinsed in fresh water before use. They have a crunchy texture and a mild but subtle flavour.

Yellow bean sauce: This thick sauce is made from crushed yellow beans, flour and salt. It is sold in cans or jars, and once the can is opened, the contents should be transferred to a screw-top jar. It will then keep in the refrigerator for months.

The wok and other utensils

By far the most frequently used cooking method in China is quick or rapid stir-frying. The best result is obtained if you use a piece of equipment known as the *wok*.

The advantage of the *wok* is that because of its shape, the heat is evenly spread to all parts of the *wok*, thus only a short cooking time is required; also the ingredients always return to the centre however vigorously you stir them. Another advantage is that only a small amount of oil is needed in comparison to a flat-bottomed frying pan. The traditional *wok* is made of iron and thus it keeps a steady and intense heat.

A new *wok* should be seasoned before use. First, wash it in hot water, then dry it by placing it over a moderate heat and wipe the inside with a pad of kitchen paper soaked in cooking oil until clean.

After each use, always wash it under hot or cold water, do not use any detergents but scrape off any food that has stuck to it with a brush or scourer. Dry thoroughly over a moderate heat before putting it away, otherwise the *wok* will rust easily.

Besides stir-frying, the *wok* can also be used for deep-frying, shallow frying, steaming, braising, stewing and boiling. The type with a single handle is best suited to stir-frying; the two-handled type is better for all other purposes, as it rests more steadily on top of a stove. The ordinary *wok* is not really suitable for an electric cooker, if you do not have gas at home, then I would strongly recommend an electric wok, a comparatively recent innovation which works well. It is also useful as a second *wok* even if you cook by gas, or for use at the table instead of a charcoal-burning fire-pot when cooking the *Chinese hot-pot* (page 70).

A Chinese bamboo steamer is another useful container to have. The advantage of a bamboo steamer over a metal one is that the bamboo lid is not absolutely airtight, thus allowing a certain amount of evaporation, which prevents condensation forming inside the lid.

A Chinese cleaver appears to be hefty, gleaming and ominously sharp, but in reality it is light, steady and not at all dangerous to use provided you handle it correctly and with care! It is one of the few essential tools for a Chinese kitchen. Once you have learnt to regard it as a cutting knife and not a chopper, you will be surprised how easy and simple it is to use compared with an ordinary kitchen knife.

The same thing can be said about using chopsticks. What appears to be hard work can be turned into great fun. If you follow a few basic rules, you just cannot go wrong. My advice is this: first relax, just don't think you are about to do something impossible, then try not to concentrate too hard on your fingers. The illustrations show how to hold and how to manipulate a pair of chopsticks.

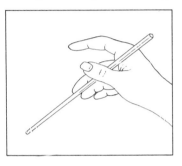

Start by placing one chopstick in the hollow between thumb and forefinger. Rest the lower end firmly below the first joint of the third finger.

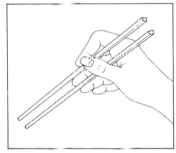

Grasp the second chopstick between your thumb and forefinger, so that its tip is level with the first.

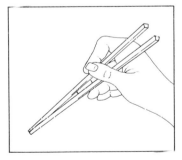

To pick up food keep the first chopstick completely steady and move only the second.

The art of menu-making

The order of different courses served at a Chinese meal depends more on the method of cooking and the way the ingredients are prepared before cooking, than the Western convention based on the soup-fish-poultry-meat-desserts-cheese sequence.

As already described, the four most important elements in Chinese cookery are colour, aroma, flavour and form. All these elements have to be well balanced to form a harmonious whole, both in a single dish and in a course of different dishes. Therefore it is quite logical that you should start your meal with light and delicate dishes and gradually work your way to rich and spicy dishes.

Another thing to remember is that the Chinese never serve an individual dish to each person, you all share the dishes on the table. The only exception is for a light snack when a dish of *Chow mein* or a bowl of *Noodles in Soup* is served, then each person is given his or her own portion.

When planning the menu for a dinner party of eight to ten people, you should start with two cold starters (or an assorted hors d'oeuvre), followed by two or three quick stir-fried dishes, then serve rice with two or three long-cooked, braised or steamed dishes, together with a soup as an optional extra. That way you will not spend all your time in the kitchen. For fewer people, you can reduce the number of dishes accordingly.

Cold starters and buffet dishes

Chinese etiquette is quite different from the Western tradition. A guest is never asked to sit at an empty table, therefore if you are going to serve one or more cold dishes as a starter, they must be on the table before you ask your guests to be seated. The great advantage of these cold dishes is that they can all be prepared and cooked well in advance (the day before if necessary), thus saving a last-minute rush.

Another advantage is that any left-overs can be saved, then served as assorted hors d'oeuvres (see pages 25 and 26). Also, the larger dishes in this section such as a whole chicken, duck or joint of meat, are ideal for buffet-style meals or party food.

You will find that almost all these cold dishes blend well with Western meals. Flexibility and diversity are two of the main aspects of the art of Chinese cooking.

Soups

Since we do not drink water at meal times in China (nor tea either, except for a small minority of people in certain parts of China), soups seem to have taken on a rather important role in an everyday meal. They act as a lubricant to help wash down the other foods and are served throughout the meal. On formal occasions or at banquets, they will appear in between courses to act as a neutralizer in order to cleanse the palate.

Chinese soups are mostly clear broths to which vegetables or meat, or both, thinly sliced or shredded, are added just before serving. All the soups in this book will serve four.

Quick stir-fried dishes

Stir-fried dishes form the backbone of everyday Chinese cooking. It is primarily a very economic way of cooking, since a great majority of these dishes only require 225 g (8 oz) meat and the same amount of vegetables, and a single dish will serve at least two people, or will stretch to accommodate 4-6 people, when combined with 2 or 3 other dishes, together with, say, a soup and rice or noodles.

Stir-frying is a quick method of cooking. All the ingredients are thinly sliced or shredded, then tossed and stirred in hot oil over a high heat for a very short time. This way meat can become well cooked in 1½-2 minutes, chicken and seafood often in less than half that time. So, provided you have selected the right materials, a simple but delicious meal of 2-3 stir-fried dishes for 4-6 people can be prepared, cooked and served in under one hour! Do all the preparation of the different dishes before you actually start the cooking.

Most stir-fried dishes consist of a main ingredient with one or several supplementary ingredients in order to give the dish the desired harmonious balance of colour, aroma, flavour, form and texture.

There are also a few deep-fried and quick-braised dishes in this section for wider variety when planning a menu.

Braised and steamed dishes

The Chinese do not normally have a sweet course to conclude a meal: after the cold starters and quick stir-fried dishes, we now settle down to what we call the big dishes, usually long-cooked and therefore most of them can be prepared and cooked well in advance, so avoiding a last-minute rush.

Some of these dishes are even interchangeable with the cold starters and buffet dishes; sometimes the distinctions are very difficult to define: the general rule is that certain dishes are best served cold, therefore they are grouped together in the first section, while a number of braised and steamed dishes are best served hot, therefore they are put in the fourth section. Again, most of these dishes blend well with Western food and almost all of them can be served either on their own as a complete meal or in conjunction with non-Chinese food.

All recipes in this section will serve 4-6 people as a main course, or will serve 8-10 as part of a multi-course Chinese meal.

Rice, noodles and pancakes

This section forms the bulk food of a Chinese meal, but most of them can be served on their own as a light meal or snack. Noodles are always served for birthday celebrations, as the Chinese regard the length of noodles as representative of long life.

Spring rolls (page 77) can be served as a starter or part of a buffet, as can the dumplings (page 78) and *Peking onion pancakes* (page 76).

Drinks

Choosing wine or wines to go with Chinese meals should not present any problems. Red or white wine can be served with a Chinese meal. The white should be dry and the red should not be too heavy. A young, fresh Beaujolais or a light claret is an ideal wine for most Chinese dishes. Of course, lager, rice wine or sake can be served if you prefer.

China tea should be served at the end of the meal without sugar or milk, it is most refreshing and invigorating.

Brillat-Savarin said that "the discovery of a new dish does more for the happiness of mankind than the discovery of a new star". I do sincerely wish that this book will bring you much happiness.

SAMPLE MENU FOR 4-6 PEOPLE

1-2 Cold Starters:
Peking poached prawns
Kidney salad
or: Assorted hors d'oeuvres (1)

1-2 Quick Stir-fried Dishes:
Fish slices with wine sauce
Shredded chicken breast with green peppers
or: Chicken cubes with celery
Cantonese beef in oyster sauce

Braised Dish to be served with rice:
'Lion's Head' (Pork meatballs with Chinese cabbage)
or: Five-spice pork spare-ribs
Egg-drop soup

Dessert:
Fresh fruit or canned lychees

SAMPLE MENU FOR 8-10 PEOPLE

2-3 Cold Starters:
Crystal-boiled prawns in jelly
Salted Peking duck
Hot and sour cabbage
or: Assorted hors d'oeuvres (2)

2-3 Quick Stir-fried Dishes:
Braised fish steak
Diced chicken in Peking bean sauce
Pork slices with Chinese vegetables

or: Red and white prawns with green vegetable
Chicken cubes with walnuts Sichuan style
Rapid-fried lamb slices

2-3 Braised or Steamed Dishes:
Lamb and cucumber soup
Aromatic and crispy Sichuan duck
Cantonese steamed sea bass
or: Steamed chicken with mushrooms
Braised beef
Fish and bean curd casserole

Dessert:
Fruit salad

COLD STARTERS & BUFFET DISHES

炝明虾
PEKING POACHED PRAWNS

225 g (8 oz) uncooked prawns
600 ml (1 pint) water
2 tablespoons rice wine or dry sherry
1 teaspoon salt
2 teaspoons sesame seed oil
1 tablespoon thinly shredded ginger root, to garnish

Preparation time: 20-25 minutes

1. If frozen, make sure the prawns are thoroughly thawed. Wash, shell and pat dry with paper towels, then cut each prawn in half lengthways.
2. Bring the water to the boil in a saucepan, then put in the prawns. When they turn white, scoop them out with a strainer and plunge them into a bowl of cold water for a few seconds. Drain well before placing them on a small serving dish.
3. Mix together the wine or sherry, salt and sesame seed oil, pour the mixture evenly over the prawns.
4. Garnish with the thinly shredded ginger root and serve cold either on its own, or as part of assorted hors d'oeuvres (pages 25 and 26).

熟炝虾仁
HOT-MIXED PRAWNS

225 g (8 oz) peeled, uncooked prawns
600 ml (1 pint) water
Sauce:
2 teaspoons cornflour
1 tablespoon water
1 tablespoon sesame seed oil
2 tablespoons soy sauce
1 teaspoon sugar
2 teaspoons finely chopped ginger root, to garnish

Preparation time: 10-15 minutes

1. Pat the prawns dry with paper towels.
2. Bring the water to the boil in a saucepan, then remove from the heat before adding the prawns. Soak the prawns for 2-3 minutes.
3. Strain the prawns and place them on a serving dish.
4. Mix the cornflour with the water to a smooth paste. Warm up the sesame seed oil in a wok or saucepan over a medium heat, then add the soy sauce and sugar. Stir until the sugar dissolves, then add the cornflour and water mixture, stirring constantly until smooth. Pour evenly over the prawns.
5. Garnish with ginger root and serve cold.

油爆虾
RAPID FRIED PRAWNS IN SHELLS

225 g (8 oz) Pacific prawns in shells, headless
oil for deep-frying
2 tablespoons rice wine or dry sherry
½ teaspoon salt
2 tablespoons soy sauce
2 teaspoons sugar
1 teaspoon finely chopped spring onions
1 teaspoon finely chopped ginger root
1 tablespoon finely chopped fresh coriander, to garnish

Preparation time: 10 minutes

This dish can be served either hot or cold. It is easier if you use chopsticks or your fingers rather than a fork to eat these prawns.

1. Wash and trim off the whiskers and legs of the prawns, but leave the shells on. Dry thoroughly.
2. Heat the oil in a wok or saucepan over a high heat until hot. Deep-fry the prawns until they turn bright red, quickly scoop them out with a strainer and pour off the oil.
3. Return the prawns to the same wok or pan, add the wine or sherry, salt, soy sauce, sugar, spring onions and ginger root, stir a few times until well blended and each prawn is coated with the glittering sauce.
4. Arrange the prawns neatly on a serving dish and garnish with fresh coriander.

CLOCKWISE FROM THE TOP: Rapid fried prawns in shells; Peking poached prawns; Hot-mixed prawns

SHANGHAI 'SMOKED' FISH

750 g (1½-1¾ lb) cod or haddock cutlets
3 tablespoons soy sauce
3 tablespoons rice wine or dry sherry
½ teaspoon salt
3-4 spring onions
3 slices ginger root, peeled
1 teaspoon five-spice powder
4 tablespoons sugar
oil for deep-frying

Preparation time: 25-30 minutes

CLOCKWISE FROM THE BOTTOM: Crystal-boiled prawns in jelly;
Jellied chicken; Fish slices in hot sauce

The interesting point about this dish is that the fish is not actually smoked. It acquires the smoky taste from being first marinated in soy sauce and wine, then deep-fried in hot oil and finally marinated again in a specially prepared sauce.

1. Leave the fish cutlets in fairly large pieces, otherwise they will break up when cooked. Marinate in the soy sauce, wine or sherry and salt for 5-10 minutes.
2. Remove the fish from the marinade. Bring the marinade to the boil in a saucepan over a moderate heat with the spring onions, ginger root, five-spice powder, sugar and about 85 ml (3 fl oz) water. Simmer gently for about 10 minutes, then strain through a sieve, reserving the sauce.
3. Heat the oil in a wok or deep-fryer until fairly hot. Deep-fry the fish pieces for about 4-5 minutes or until they are crisp and golden. Remove with a perforated spoon and dip them in the sauce for 10 minutes or so before laying them out side by side on a plate to cool. The remainder of the sauce can be stored in the refrigerator for 3-4 weeks and used again.

珊瑚魚片
FISH SLICES IN HOT SAUCE

450 g (1 lb) fish fillet (cod or haddock)
2 tablespoons rice wine or dry sherry
1 teaspoon salt
300 ml (½ pint) oil
1 medium red pepper, cored, seeded and shredded
100 g (4 oz) bamboo shoots, sliced
2-3 spring onions, cut into short lengths
2 slices ginger root, peeled and shredded
1 teaspoon sugar
120 ml (4 fl oz) Stock (page 28)
2 teaspoons chilli sauce

Preparation time: 15-20 minutes

This is a very colourful dish with a piquant taste. It can be served hot or cold.

1. Cut the fish fillet into about 12 slices, marinate in the wine or sherry and ½ teaspoon of the salt for 10 minutes.
2. Heat the oil in a wok or frying pan, put in the fish slices piece by piece and fry for 2-3 minutes. Gently lift the fish out and drain on absorbent paper.
3. Pour off most of the oil, leaving about 1 tablespoon in the wok, add the red pepper, bamboo shoots, spring onions and ginger root. Stir a few times, then add the remaining salt, sugar and stock. Bring it to the boil, put the fish slices in and reduce to a low heat.
4. When the juice is almost all evaporated, add the chilli sauce and let it blend before carefully removing the fish slices to a serving dish.

凍雞
JELLIED CHICKEN

1½ kg (3-3½ lb) roasting chicken
2 litres (3½ pints) water
3 spring onions
3 slices ginger root
2 teaspoons salt
2 tablespoons rice wine or dry sherry

Preparation time: 25-30 minutes, plus setting
Cooking time: 1¾ hours

水晶明虾
CRYSTAL-BOILED PRAWNS IN JELLY

225 g (8 oz) peeled prawns
300 ml (½ pint) Stock (page 28)
2 slices ginger root, peeled
1 spring onion
1 teaspoon Sichuan or black peppercorns
1 teaspoon salt
Jelly:
2 teaspoons gelatine
150 ml (¼ pint) hot water
To garnish:
a few thin slices of cucumber

Preparation time: 25-30 minutes, plus setting

This is a very attractive dish, ideal for hors d'oeuvres or as part of a buffet.

1. Place the prawns in a saucepan with the stock, ginger root, spring onion, peppercorns and salt; bring to the boil, turn down the heat and simmer gently for about 5 minutes.
2. Take the prawns out and cut each one in half lengthways. Arrange them in neat layers on a dish or in a jelly mould.
3. Strain the stock and discard the solid ingredients. Dissolve the gelatine in the hot water and add the strained stock.
4. Pour the gelatine over the prawns and leave to cool, then refrigerate until set.
5. To serve, turn the jelly out on to another dish and decorate the edge of the plate with thinly sliced cucumber pieces.

1. Boil the chicken in the water in a saucepan for about 1 hour. Remove the chicken, reserving the stock. Take the meat off the bone, skin and place the meat in a pudding basin.
2. Cover the meat with the cooking stock, add the spring onions, ginger root, salt and wine or sherry, plus the chicken skin.
3. Place the basin in a steamer or double saucepan and steam the chicken vigorously for at least 45 minutes. Remove the basin, discard the skin, spring onions and ginger root.
4. When the basin is cool, place it in the refrigerator for 6-8 hours to set.
5. To serve, turn the basin on to a plate. The juice will have set as a delicious jelly.
6. The chicken bones can be used for making a stock in the remaining liquid.

豉 油 鷄 (廣東式)

CANTONESE SOYA BRAISED CHICKEN

1½ kg (3-3½ lb) roasting chicken
2 tablespoons freshly ground Sichuan or black pepper
2 tablespoons finely chopped ginger root
5 tablespoons dark soy sauce
3 tablespoons rice wine or dry sherry
2 tablespoons sugar
3 tablespoons oil
120 ml (4 fl oz) water or Stock (page 28)
1 small lettuce

Preparation time: 15 minutes, plus marinating
Cooking time: 50 minutes

LEFT TO RIGHT: Soya duck; Sichuan bang-bang chicken

This is the bright brown chicken seen in the windows of Chinese restaurants. It can be served hot or cold.

1. Clean the chicken well and dry it thoroughly. Rub both inside and out with the pepper and ginger root.
2. Marinate the bird in the soy sauce, wine or sherry and sugar for at least 45 minutes, turning it over several times.
3. Heat the oil in a wok or a pan large enough to hold the whole chicken. Brown it lightly all over, then add the marinade diluted with the water or stock. Bring it to the boil, reduce the heat, cover and leave to simmer for 45 minutes, turning it over several times during cooking (being careful not to break the skin).
4. Chop the chicken into small pieces and arrange them neatly on a bed of lettuce leaves, then pour over 2 tablespoons of the sauce to serve when cold. The remainder of the sauce can be stored in the refrigerator for 3-4 weeks and used again.

棒 棒 鳮

SICHUAN BANG-BANG CHICKEN

175 g (6 oz) chicken breast meat, boned and skinned
1 lettuce heart
Sauce:
1 tablespoon sesame sauce
1 tablespoon light soy sauce
2 teaspoons vinegar
1 teaspoon chilli sauce
1 teaspoon sugar
2 tablespoons Stock (page 28)

Preparation time: 15-20 minutes

This popular dish served in Peking and Sichuan restaurants is extremely simple to cook. If you cannot get sesame sauce (sometimes called sesame paste), an acceptable substitute is peanut butter creamed with a little sesame seed oil.

1. Cover the chicken meat with cold water in a saucepan and bring to the boil, then reduce the heat and simmer gently for 10 minutes. Remove the chicken and beat it with a rolling pin until soft – hence the name of the dish.
2. Cut the lettuce leaves into shreds and place them on a serving dish. Pull the chicken meat into shreds with your fingers and place on top of the lettuce leaves.
3. Mix together all the ingredients for the sauce and pour evenly over the chicken to serve when cold.

芥 末 鳮 絲

SHREDDED CHICKEN IN MUSTARD SAUCE

1 pair of chicken breasts, boned and skinned
½ teaspoon salt
2 egg whites
1 tablespoon cornflour
150 ml (¼ pint) oil
Sauce:
2 tablespoons mustard powder (see method)
1 tablespoon light soy sauce
1 tablespoon vinegar
2 teaspoons sesame seed oil

Preparation time: 30 minutes

醬 鴨

SOYA DUCK

2 kg (4½-4¾ lb) duckling
1.2 litres (2 pints) water
2 teaspoons salt
4 spring onions
4 slices ginger root
1 teaspoon five-spice powder
3 tablespoons rice wine or dry sherry
6 tablespoons dark soy sauce
100 g (4 oz) crystallized brown sugar
1 tablespoon sesame seed oil

Preparation time: 30 minutes
Cooking time: 2 hours

1. Clean the duck well, cut off and discard the 'parson's nose'. Reserve the giblets for *Drunken giblets* (page 20).
2. Bring the water to the boil in a large saucepan, blanch the duck for 1 minute, then dry it thoroughly both inside and out. Rub about 1 teaspoon of the salt inside it.
3. Add the remaining salt, spring onions, ginger root and five-spice powder to the pan and bring to the boil.
4. Return the duck to the pot and add the wine or sherry, soy sauce and sugar. Cover and simmer gently for 1½ hours, then lift the duck out and rub it all over with sesame seed oil.
5. Boil the cooking liquid uncovered, reducing it a little, then use it to baste the duck several times before chopping the meat into small pieces (see page 8). Serve hot or cold.

Mix English mustard powder with cold water to form a thin paste and let it mellow for about 30 minutes before using.

1. Thinly shred the chicken and mix with the salt, egg whites and cornflour.
2. Heat the oil in a preheated wok or frying pan, stir in the chicken over a medium heat. Separate the chicken shreds with chopsticks or a fork. As soon as their colour changes to pale white, scoop out with a perforated spoon and drain, then place on a serving dish.
3. Mix all the ingredients for the sauce together thoroughly and pour evenly over the chicken. Serve cold.

醉 鴨 肫

DRUNKEN GIBLETS

giblets (see recipe) from 2-3 ducks or chicken
2 tablespoons rice wine or dry sherry
1 tablespoon brandy
1 teaspoon salt
1 tablespoon sugar
120 ml (4 fl oz) Stock (page 28)
1 teaspoon thinly shredded ginger root, to garnish

Preparation time: 15-20 minutes

In cooking terms, giblets consist of the head, neck, heart, wing tips, feet, gizzard, kidneys and liver of the poultry. These are normally used for making stock but can make excellent dishes in their own right.

1. For this dish, you only need to use the gizzard, heart and liver. Clean and trim them thoroughly. Make sure that the dark green-coloured gall bladder is not broken, when removed from the liver, otherwise it will leave a sharp bitter taste.
2. Place the cleaned giblets in a saucepan with cold water to cover and slowly bring to the boil, this is important as rapid boiling will toughen them, particularly the liver. After simmering for 5-6 minutes, take them out and cut into thin slices (discarding the water).
3. Place the giblets in a clean pan and add the wine or sherry, brandy, salt, sugar and stock. Bring to the boil slowly as before and simmer for 10 minutes, then leave to cool in the juice.
4. To serve, take out and drain the sliced giblets, then garnish with thinly shredded ginger root.

鹽 水 鴨

SALTED PEKING DUCK

2 kg (4½-4¾ lb) duckling
1.75 litres (3 pints) water
2 spring onions
1 tablespoon Sichuan or black peppercorns
1 tablespoon salt
3 slices ginger root
3 tablespoons rice wine or dry sherry

Preparation time: 10-15 minutes, plus cooling
Cooking time: 1¼ hours

滷 肚 片

BRAISED TRIPE

750 g (1½-1¾ lb) tripe
2 tablespoons oil
2 slices ginger root
2 spring onions
1 teaspoon five-spice powder
3 tablespoons rice wine or dry sherry
4 tablespoons soy sauce
1 tablespoon sugar
1 litre (1¾ pints) Stock (page 28)
To garnish:
2 teaspoons sesame seed oil
1 teaspoon finely chopped fresh coriander or spring onions

Preparation time: 5-10 minutes
Cooking time: 1½ hours

This is another dish which can be served cold as a starter, or hot as a main course.

1. The tripe you buy in this country normally has already been thoroughly cleaned and treated. Just pat it dry with paper towels, then heat the oil in a hot saucepan and brown the tripe lightly. Add all the remaining ingredients and bring to the boil. (If you have any sauce left from *Soya duck* (page 19) or *Spiced beef* (page 22), it can be used here instead of or in addition to the stock.)
2. Lower the heat, cover and simmer gently for 1¼ hours.
3. Remove the tripe, cut it into small pieces and place on a serving dish. Garnish with the sesame seed oil and fresh coriander or spring onions.

The duck must be cooked whole to keep the skin intact. If the water comes in contact with the meat it will toughen it. Use the leftover bones for stock.

1. Clean the duck well, reserving the giblets for use in *Drunken giblets* (above). Place it in a large saucepan and cover with the cold water. Bring to the boil over a medium heat, cover and simmer for 1 hour.
2. Take the duck out, reserving the liquid and remove all the meat from the bone.
3. Place the meat in a smaller pan, add the spring onions, peppercorns, salt, ginger root, wine or sherry and 150 ml (¼ pint) of the cooking liquid.
4. Cover and cook over a high heat for 10 minutes. Remove and leave to cool.
5. To serve, take the meat out and cut it into thin slices or strips. Strain the juice and pour it over the duck.

炮 腰 花

KIDNEY SALAD

1 pair pig's kidney (about 225 g/8 oz)
600 ml (1 pint) boiling water
2 slices ginger root, peeled and thinly shredded
Sauce:
½ teaspoon salt
2 tablespoons rice wine or dry sherry
1 tablespoon sesame seed oil
To garnish:
1 spring onion, chopped

Preparation time: 15-20 minutes, plus marinating

1. Peel off the thin white skin covering the kidneys. Split them in half lengthways and discard the fat and tough white parts in the middle. Score the surface of the kidneys diagonally in a criss-cross pattern, then cut them into thin slices.
2. Place the slices in a saucepan with the boiling water over a medium heat to blanch. Do not overcook: as soon as the water starts to reboil, remove the kidneys and drain, then run cold water over them for a few seconds before placing on a serving dish.
3. Combine the thinly shredded ginger root with the kidney slices. Mix together the ingredients for the sauce and pour evenly over the slices. Leave to marinate for at least 10-15 minutes before garnishing with spring onion and serving cold.

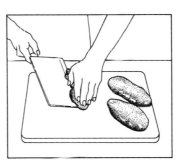 

If the kidneys still have their covering of white skin, peel this off, then split them in half lengthways.

Discard the white core in the middle of each half. Score the outside of each piece in a criss-cross pattern by making deep diagonal cuts in two directions.

TOP TO BOTTOM: Kidney salad; Braised tripe

酸辣白菜

HOT AND SOUR CABBAGE

450 g (1 lb) white cabbage
1 green pepper, cored and seeded
1 red pepper, cored and seeded
2 tablespoons soy sauce
2 tablespoons vinegar
2 tablespoons sugar
1 teaspoon salt
3 tablespoons oil
4-6 dried hot chillis
12 Sichuan or black peppercorns
1 tablespoon sesame seed oil, to garnish

Preparation time: 15-20 minutes

1. Thinly shred the cabbage and the green and red peppers.
2. Mix together the soy sauce, vinegar, sugar and salt to make the sauce.
3. Heat the oil in a preheated wok or a large frying pan and add the dried chillis and peppercorns. After a few seconds, add the cabbage and the green and red peppers. Stir for 1-1½ minutes, then pour in the sauce mixture and continue stirring untill well blended.
4. Serve either hot or cold garnished with sesame seed oil.

白切肉

CRYSTAL-BOILED PORK WITH DIP-SAUCE

750 g (1½-1¾ lb) leg of pork, boned but not skinned
Sauce:
4 tablespoons soy sauce
1 tablespoon sesame seed oil
1 teaspoon finely chopped spring onion
1 teaspoon finely chopped ginger root
½ teaspoon finely chopped garlic
1 teaspoon chilli sauce (optional)

Preparation time: 15-20 minutes
Cooking time: 1¼ hours

五香滷牛肉

SPICED BEEF

750 g (1½-1¾ lb) shin of beef
4 slices ginger root
3 tablespoons rice wine or dry sherry
1 tablespoon brandy
2 tablespoons oil
4 tablespoons soy sauce
1 tablespoon sugar
1 teaspoon five-spice powder

Preparation time: 10-15 minutes
Cooking time: about 1½ hours

1. Place the beef with the ginger root in a saucepan, add the wine or sherry and brandy and cover with water. Bring to the boil, skimming off the scum, cover and simmer gently for 45 minutes.
2. Take the beef out, reserving the cooking liquid. Cut the beef into large chunks, then fry in hot oil. Add the soy sauce, sugar and five-spice powder with about half of the cooking liquid.
3. Cover and simmer for 40-45 minutes. Serve thinly sliced either hot or cold.

1. Place the pork in one piece (tied together with string if necessary) in a saucepan of boiling water. Skim off the scum, cover and simmer gently for 1 hour, then remove and soak the meat in cold water for about 1 minute.
2. To serve, remove the string and cut off the skin, leaving a thin layer of fat on top. Cut the meat into small thin slices across the grain. Put any uneven pieces in the centre of a serving dish, arrange some of the slices in two meat rows on either side and then neatly arrange the remainder in a third row on top, so that it resembles an arched bridge.
3. Mix together all the ingredients for the sauce, then either pour evenly over the meat, or serve separately as a dip-sauce.

CLOCKWISE FROM THE BOTTOM: Hot and sour cabbage; Braised bean-curd; Crystal-boiled pork with dip-sauce

滷 豆 腐

BRAISED BEAN CURD

4 cakes of bean curd
175 g (6 oz) pork spare ribs
2 spring onions
2 slices ginger root, peeled
50 g (2 oz) bacon or pork fat
3 tablespoons soy sauce
1 tablespoon sugar
2 tablespoons rice wine or dry sherry

Preparation time: 10-15 minutes
Cooking time: 45 minutes

1. Place the bean curd in a saucepan, cover with cold water. Bring to the boil, cover and cook over a high heat for 10 minutes, when the texture of the bean curd will resemble a beehive.
2. Cut the spare ribs into small pieces, then cook them with the spring onions and ginger root in about 300 ml (½ pint) water for 5 minutes.
3. Place the bacon or pork fat at the bottom of another saucepan, then place the bean curd on top and add the spare ribs. Add the soy sauce, sugar, wine or sherry and the water in which the spare ribs have been cooking, together with the spring onions and ginger root. Bring to the boil, cover and simmer gently for 30 minutes. Turn off the heat and leave to cool.
4. To serve, discard the spare ribs, take the bean curd out and cut it into small pieces.

莱 松

CRISPY 'SEAWEED'

750 g (1½-1¾ lb) spring greens
oil for deep-frying
1 teaspoon salt
1½ teaspoons caster sugar

Preparation time: 10 minutes, plus drying

You might be surprised or even shocked to learn that the very popular 'seaweed' served in Chinese restaurants is, in fact, green cabbage! Although we do not eat real seaweed in China, this is an authentic recipe originating from Peking. Choose fresh, young spring greens with pointed heads before the hearts are developed into hard, rounded cabbages, even the deep green outer leaves are quite tender. This recipe also makes an ideal garnish for a number of dishes, particularly cold starters and buffet dishes.

1. Wash and dry the spring green leaves, shred with a sharp knife into the thinnest possible shavings. Spread them out on absorbent paper or put in a large colander to dry thoroughly for about 30 minutes.
2. Heat the oil in a wok or deep-fryer, but before it gets too hot, turn off the heat for ½ minute. Add the spring green shavings in several batches and turn the heat up to medium high. Stir with cooking chopsticks and when the shavings start to float to the surface, scoop them out gently with a slotted spoon and drain on absorbent paper, to remove as much of the oil as possible.
3. Sprinkle the salt and caster sugar evenly on top, then mix gently. Serve cold.

Variation:

Deep-fry 50 g (2 oz) split almonds until crisp and add to the 'seaweed' as a garnish, to give the dish a new dimension.

糖 醋 黄 瓜

SWEET AND SOUR CUCUMBER

1 cucumber
1 teaspoon salt
2 tablespoons caster sugar
2 tablespoons vinegar

Preparation time: 25-30 minutes

Select a dark green cucumber that is slender rather than fat and overgrown. The large, pale green ones contain too much water and have far less flavour.

1. Split the cucumber in half lengthways, then cut it into strips rather like potato chips. Marinate with the salt for about 10 minutes, to extract the bitter juices.
2. Remove the cucumber chips and give each one a gentle pat with the blade of a cleaver or knife.
3. Place them on a serving dish. Sprinkle first the sugar evenly over them and then the vinegar.

Crispy 'seaweed' with split almonds; Sweet and sour cucumber

三色拼盤

ASSORTED HORS D'OEUVRES (1)

---

100 g (4 oz) Rapid-fried prawns in shells (page 14)
100 g (4 oz) Sichuan bang-bang chicken (page 19)
100 g (4 oz) Spiced beef, thinly sliced (page 22)
Crispy 'seaweed' (page 24) or ½ cucumber, thinly sliced, to
   garnish

Instead of serving several different dishes separately at the start of a meal, a selection of thinly sliced cooked meats, neatly arranged on a large plate with some colourful garnishes, always looks attractive and appealing. This assorted hors d'oeuvre consists of only three basic ingredients: fish, chicken and meat. Similar types of food can be substituted, but always bear in mind the Chinese principles of harmony, contrast and balance both in colour and flavour.

1. Arrange each of the ingredients neatly in separate rows on a serving dish (never mix them, as this will spoil the appearance), garnish the edge of the plate with either the 'seaweed' or cucumber slices.
2. All the cooking can be done hours, if not days, before, so if you can have this dish prepared long before your guests arrive, you will save yourself a last-minute rush.

什 錦 冷 盤

ASSORTED HORS D'OEUVRES (2)

This is a more elaborate version of the previous recipe; again the ingredients are chosen for their harmonious contrast and balance in colour, flavour and texture. Because of the large number of different ingredients used in this recipe, quantities of each item are not given, so that you can adapt it to suit the occasion. As a guide, using 50 g (2 oz) of each item should serve at least 8-10 people.

Here is a list of suggestions, you may substitute any other ingredients you happen to have in your kitchen, just use your ingenuity and imagination, create your own variations to astonish your guests. Only remember not to have more than one of the same type of food.

1. Hot mixed prawns (page 14)
2. Shanghai 'smoked' fish (page 16)
3. Shredded chicken in mustard sauce (page 19)
4. Soya duck (page 19)
5. Braised tripe (page 20)
6. Crystal-boiled pork (page 22)
7. Braised bean curd (page 23)
8. Sweet and sour cucumber (page 24)

To garnish:
tomatoes, spring onions, radishes or lettuce hearts

To make radish garnishes, choose a bunch of largish, evenly sized radishes. Using a sharp knife, make several cuts on each of the radishes about two-thirds of the way down but not all the way through.

Put the radishes in a large jar. Add ½ teaspoon salt and 1½ teaspoons sugar, then shake the jar well, so that each radish is coated with the mixture. Leave to marinate for several hours or overnight. Just before serving, pour off the liquid and spread out each radish like a fan.

To make spring onion flowers, trim both ends, so that the stalk measures about 7.5 cm/3 inches in length. Use a sharp knife to shred the green part to within 2.5 cm/1 inch of the white stem. Plunge the onions into iced water for about 1 hour. Drain and pat dry before use. They can be left in water for several hours.

TOP: Soya duck; Crystal-boiled pork; Shanghai 'smoked' fish

BOTTOM: OUTSIDE RING CLOCKWISE FROM LEFT: Sweet and sour cucumber; Braised bean-curd; Shanghai 'smoked' fish; Crystal-boiled pork

INNER RING: CLOCKWISE FROM LEFT: Hot-mixed prawns; Shredded chicken in mustard sauce; Braised tripe

SOUPS

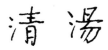

THE BASIC STOCK FOR SOUPS

Makes 2 litres (3½ pints)
1½-1¾ kg (3-4 lb) boiling chicken or pork spare ribs
2.75 litres (5 pints) water
4-6 slices ginger root
3-4 spring onions

Cooking time: 2-2½ hours

1. Place all the ingredients in a large saucepan – there is no need to peel the ginger root or cut the spring onions, as they are discarded after cooking. Bring to the boil, skimming off any scum. Reduce the heat, cover and simmer gently for 2-2½ hours.
2. Strain the stock when cool (after 2-3 hours), then refrigerate. The chicken carcass has given up its flavour to the stock during the long cooking and is not worth keeping.
3. Remove the solidified fat from the top of the stock before use. The stock will keep in the refrigerator for at least a week, after that boil it every 2 or 3 days.

SLICED PORK AND CABBAGE SOUP

100 g (4 oz) pork steak
1 tablespoon rice wine or dry sherry
1 tablespoon soy sauce
100 g (4 oz) Chinese cabbage
600 ml (1 pint) Stock (page 28)
1 teaspoon salt

Preparation time: 15 minutes, plus marinating

1. Thinly slice the pork. Marinate in the wine or sherry and soy sauce for 10 minutes.
2. Cut the cabbage in 2½ cm (1 inch) lengths.
3. Bring the stock to the boil, add the pork, stirring to keep the slices separate. Boil for 30 seconds, add the cabbage and salt, reduce the heat and simmer for 1½-2 minutes.

LEFT TO RIGHT: Sliced pork and cabbage soup;
Chinese mushroom soup

CHINESE MUSHROOM SOUP

6 medium Chinese dried mushrooms or 100 g (4 oz) fresh
    mushrooms (preferably black field mushrooms)
2 teaspoons cornflour
1 tablespoon cold water
3 egg whites
2 teaspoons salt
600 ml (1 pint) Stock (page 28)
1 teaspoon finely chopped spring onion, to garnish

Preparation time: 10-15 minutes, plus soaking

1. Soak the dried mushrooms in warm water for 20-30 minutes, then squeeze dry, discard the hard stalks and cut into thin slices. If using fresh mushrooms, wash (do not peel) and slice them.
2. Mix the cornflour with the water. Comb the egg whites with your fingers to loosen them (do not use a whisk as too much air will make them frothy) and add a pinch of the salt.
3. Bring the stock to the boil and add the mushrooms. Boil together for 1 minute, then add the cornflour, stirring constantly.
4. Add the remaining salt and pour the egg white very slowly into the soup, stirring all the time.
5. Garnish with the spring onions and serve hot.

EGG-DROP SOUP

2 eggs
1 teaspoon salt
600 ml (1 pint) Stock (page 28)
2 teaspoons finely chopped spring onion, to garnish

Preparation time: 5 minutes

1. Beat the eggs with a pinch of the salt.
2. Bring the stock to the boil, pour the beaten eggs in very slowly, stirring constantly.
3. Place the remaining salt and spring onions in a serving bowl, pour in the soup and serve hot.

一品豆腐湯

BEAN CURD SOUP

2 cakes bean curd
100 g (4 oz) crab meat, fresh or canned
1 bunch watercress
600 ml (1 pint) Stock (page 28)
1 teaspoon salt

Preparation time: 10 minutes

1. Cut each cake of bean curd into about 20 small cubes.
2. Break the crab meat into small pieces. Wash the watercress.
3. Bring the stock to the boil, add the salt, bean curd cubes and crab meat. Boil for 1 minute.
4. Place the watercress in a large serving bowl and pour the soup over it. Stir and serve hot.

汆肝片湯

LIVER SOUP

100 g (4 oz) pig's liver
1 teaspoon cornflour
100 g (4 oz) spinach leaves
600 ml (1 pint) Stock (page 28)
1 teaspoon salt
1 tablespoon soy sauce
1 teaspoon sesame seed oil, to garnish

Preparation time: 10-15 minutes

1. Thinly slice the liver and cut into small pieces about the size of a postage stamp. Mix with the cornflour.
2. Wash the spinach and cut the large leaves into 2 or 3 pieces.
3. Bring the stock to the boil, add the liver, spinach, salt and soy sauce. Boil for 1 minute.
4. Add the sesame seed oil and serve hot.

魚片湯
SLICED FISH SOUP

225 g (8 oz) fish fillet (plaice or sole)
1 egg white
1 tablespoon cornflour
1 lettuce heart
600 ml (1 pint) Stock (page 28)
salt
freshly ground white pepper
1 teaspoon finely chopped spring onion, to garnish

Preparation time: 15-20 minutes

1. Cut the fish fillet into large slices about the size of a matchbox, mix with the egg white and cornflour. Thinly shred the lettuce heart.
2. Bring the stock to the boil, add the salt and fish slices. Simmer for 1 minute.
3. Place the shredded lettuce in a large serving bowl, add plenty of white pepper and pour the soup over it. Garnish with spring onions and serve hot.

魚丸湯
FISH BALLS WITH VEGETABLE SOUP

100 g (4 oz) fish balls (see recipe)
50 g (2 oz) mushrooms
50 g (2 oz) cooked ham
50 g (2 oz) bamboo shoots
600 ml (1 pint) Stock (page 28)
salt
chopped fresh coriander leaves, to garnish

Preparation time: 10-15 minutes (1-1¼ hours if making the fish balls)

Fish balls can be bought ready-made from oriental stores, or you can make your own. To make fish balls, finely mince 100 g (4 oz) fresh fish fillet (such as cod or haddock), beat in a mixer with 1 well-beaten egg, 1 tablespoon cornflour and a few drops of vegetable oil for 5-10 minutes. Chill the mixture for about 1 hour to harden it, then make into walnut-size balls.

1. Thinly slice the mushrooms, ham and bamboo shoots.
2. Bring the stock to a fast boil, add the fish balls one by one and as soon as they float to the surface, add the mushrooms, ham, bamboo shoots and salt. Cook for 1 minute.
3. Pour the soup into a serving bowl, add the fresh coriander leaves to garnish and serve hot.

The Chinese traditionally make marvellous soups merely by stir-frying a handful of fresh greens or whatever is at hand, adding some water and seasoning and bringing it to a rapid boil. If you have some ready-made stock, there is no limit to what you can make into an instantly prepared soup. In China the very best stock is made from a whole chicken, a whole duck and a leg of ham or pork. Of course, you can make a perfectly good stock by following the recipe on page 28.

A chicken stock cube made up with 600 ml (1 pint) water can be substituted, but the flavour will not be as good. Also remember that a stock cube (chicken or beef) is salted, while the home-made stock is not, so adjust seasoning accordingly.

LEFT TO RIGHT: Liver soup; Sliced fish soup; Fish balls with vegetable soup

三 鮮 湯

THREE-FLAVOURS (PORK, CHICKEN AND PRAWN) SOUP

100 g (4 oz) pork fillet
100 g (4 oz) chicken breast meat, skinned and boned
100 g (4 oz) prawns, peeled
600 ml (1 pint) Stock (page 28)
about 1½ teaspoons salt

Preparation time: 20-25 minutes

1. Thinly slice the pork and chicken meat and cut into small pieces. If the prawns are large, cut them into 2 or 3 pieces each.
2. Bring the stock to the boil, add the pork, chicken, prawns and salt. Cook for 1-1½ minutes.
3. Serve hot either in a large bowl or ladle into 4 individual soup bowls, adjusting the seasoning to taste.

Variation:
Any other kind of shell fish, such as scallops, crab meat, lobster, oyster or abalone, can be substituted for the prawns.

羊 肉 黃 瓜 湯

LAMB AND CUCUMBER SOUP

225 g (8 oz) leg of lamb fillet
1 tablespoon rice wine or dry sherry
1 tablespoon soy sauce
½ cucumber
600 ml (1 pint) Stock (page 28)
salt
1 teaspoon finely chopped spring onion, to garnish

Preparation time: 15-20 minutes

1. Thinly slice the lamb and cut into small pieces, about the size of a large postage stamp. Marinate them in the wine or sherry and soy sauce for 10 minutes.
2. Thinly slice the cucumber, do not peel.
3. Bring the stock to the boil, add the lamb, cucumber and salt, stir and continue cooking for 1½-2 minutes.
4. Place the spring onions in a serving bowl, pour over the soup and serve hot.

LEFT TO RIGHT: Chicken and ham soup; Lamb and cucumber soup; Eight-treasure soup

鷄 絲 火 腿 湯

CHICKEN AND HAM SOUP

100 g (4 oz) chicken breast meat, skinned and boned
100 g (4 oz) cooked ham
600 ml (1 pint) Stock (page 28)
1 teaspoon finely chopped spring onion, to garnish
1 teaspoon salt

Preparation time: 10-15 minutes

1. Thinly slice the chicken and ham and cut into small pieces.
2. Bring the stock to the boil, add the chicken and ham slices. Cook for 1 minute.
3. Place the spring onions and salt in a serving bowl, pour in the soup and serve hot.

八宝湯

EIGHT-TREASURE SOUP

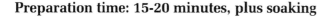

50 g (2 oz) prawns, peeled *or* 1 tablespoon dried shrimps
50 g (2 oz) chicken breast meat, skinned and boned
50 g (2 oz) pork fillet
50 g (2 oz) bamboo shoots
1 egg
salt
50 g (2 oz) spinach leaves
1 cake of bean curd
2 medium tomatoes, skinned
750 ml (1¼ pints) Stock (page 28)
1 tablespoon soy sauce
1 tablespoon cornflour mixed with 1 tablespoon water
freshly ground pepper
1 teaspoon finely chopped spring onion, to garnish

Preparation time: 15-20 minutes, plus soaking

This soup is for special occasions such as a New Year Feast, or birthday celebrations. The ingredients can be varied according to seasonal availability, bearing in mind the appeal of colour and textural contrast.

1. If using dried shrimps, soak them in warm water for 20 minutes, then drain. Thinly shred the chicken, pork and bamboo shoots. Beat the egg with a pinch of salt. Thinly shred the spinach, bean curd and tomatoes.
2. Bring the stock to the boil, put in the prawns or shrimps, chicken and pork. When they start to float to the surface, pour in the beaten egg gently, then add the soy sauce and all the vegetables. Cook for about 1 minute.
3. Thicken the soup with the cornflour and water mixture. Add salt and pepper to taste and garnish with the spring onions. Serve hot.

QUICK STIR-FRIED DISHES

甜 酸 排 骨

PORK SPARE RIBS IN CANTONESE SWEET AND SOUR SAUCE

450 g (1 lb) pork spare ribs
½ teaspoon salt
freshly ground Sichuan or black pepper
1 teaspoon sugar
1 egg yolk
1 tablespoon cornflour
1 small green pepper, cored and seeded
1 small red pepper, cored and seeded
oil for deep frying
2 tablespoons plain flour
Sauce:
1 tablespoon soy sauce
3 tablespoons sugar
3 tablespoons vinegar
1 tablespoon cornflour mixed with 3 tablespoons water

Preparation time: 15-20 minutes, plus marinating

The sauce is bright and translucent, not too sweet nor too sour, and the meat succulent.

1. Chop each spare rib into 2 or 3 pieces. Place them in a bowl and add the salt, pepper, sugar, egg yolk and cornflour. Mix well together and leave to marinate for about 10 minutes.
2. Thinly shred the green and red peppers.
3. Heat the oil in a wok or deep saucepan until hot, then turn down the heat to low and let the oil cool a little. Coat each spare rib piece in plain flour before deep frying them. Put them in the oil piece by piece, so that they do not stick together, separating them with chopsticks if necessary. Increase the heat to high after a while and fry until crisp and golden, then remove with a perforated spoon.
4. Heat the oil until bubbling and fry the spare ribs once more for about 30 seconds, or until golden brown. Remove with a perforated spoon and drain.
5. Pour off most of the oil, leaving about 1 tablespoon in the wok or pan and stir-fry the green and red peppers for a few seconds. Add the soy sauce, sugar and vinegar, stir a few times, then add the cornflour mixed with water, stirring continuously. When the sauce becomes a smooth paste, put in the spare ribs, blend well and serve immediately.

滑 溜 里 脊 片

PORK SLICES WITH CHINESE VEGETABLES

225 g (8 oz) pork fillet
1 tablespoon soy sauce
1 tablespoon rice wine or dry sherry
1 tablespoon cornflour
100 g (4 oz) bamboo shoots
15 g (½ oz) wooden ears
100 g (4 oz) mange-tout peas or broccoli
100 g (4 oz) water chestnuts
2 spring onions
4 tablespoons oil
1 teaspoon salt
1 teaspoon sugar
1 teaspoon sesame seed oil

Preparation time: 25-30 minutes

1. Cut the pork into thin slices about the size of large postage stamps, then mix with the soy sauce, wine or sherry and ½ tablespoon of the cornflour.
2. Cut the bamboo shoots into roughly the same size as the pork. Soak the wooden ears in warm water for 10-15 minutes, rinse in fresh water and discard the hard stalks, then cut them into small pieces. Top and tail the mange-tout peas and leave whole, if they are small, otherwise snap them in half. If using broccoli cut it into small pieces, too. Cut each water chestnut into 2 or 3 pieces and cut the spring onions into short lengths.
3. Heat up the oil in a preheated wok or frying pan, stir-fry the pork over a high heat for about 1 minute or until the colour changes. Scoop out with a perforated spoon and set aside.
4. In the remaining hot oil, stir-fry the spring onions, followed by the mange-touts or broccoli. (As broccoli takes longer to cook, allow an extra minute or so before adding the remaining ingredients.) Add the bamboo shoots, wooden ears and water chestnuts. Next add the salt and sugar, stir a few more times, then add the pork, stirring for about 1 minute, followed by the remaining cornflour mixed with a little water and blend well. Finally, add the sesame seed oil and serve hot.

Pork spare ribs in Cantonese sweet and sour sauce; Pork slices with Chinese vegetables

豉 椒 牛 肉

BEEF AND GREEN PEPPERS IN CANTONESE BLACK BEAN SAUCE

225-275 g (8-10 oz) beef frying steak
¼ teaspoon salt
1 tablespoon soy sauce
1 tablespoon rice wine or dry sherry
1 teaspoon sugar
1 tablespoon cornflour
100 g (4 oz) green pepper, cored and seeded
100 g (4 oz) onions, peeled
2 slices ginger root, peeled
2 spring onions
1-2 green or red chillis
4 tablespoons oil
1½ tablespoons salted black beans crushed in 1 tablespoon rice wine or dry sherry

Preparation time: 20-25 minutes

Though pork is undoubtedly the most popular meat in China, beef is an important part of the daily diet of the Chinese Moslems, who number about 4 million and are widely distributed throughout China.

1. Cut the beef into thin slices about the size of a large postage stamp, then mix them with the salt, soy sauce, wine or sherry, sugar and cornflour.
2. Slice the green peppers and onions into roughly the same size as the beef. Cut the ginger root, spring onions and chillis into thin shreds.
3. Heat the oil in a preheated wok or frying pan until smoking, quickly stir-fry the beef slices for a few seconds, then remove with a perforated spoon. In the same oil, add the ginger root, spring onions, chillis, green peppers and onions. Stir a few times, then add the crushed black bean mixture and beef and blend well together. Cook for 1 minute at the most and serve immediately.

Variation:
A black bean sauce can be purchased but will not have the same flavour as the crushed bean and wine mixture. Use the same amount.

干 炒 牛 肉 絲

SICHUAN DRY-FRIED SHREDDED BEEF

275 g (10 oz) beef frying steak
100 g (4 oz) carrots
2 tablespoons sesame seed oil
2 tablespoons rice wine or dry sherry
1 tablespoon chilli bean paste
1 tablespoon Hoi Sin sauce or barbecue sauce
1 clove garlic, crushed and finely chopped
½ teaspoon salt
1 tablespoon sugar
2 spring onions, finely chopped
2 slices ginger root, peeled and finely chopped
½ teaspoon freshly ground Sichuan or black pepper
1 teaspoon chilli oil

Preparation time: 20-25 minutes

Dry-frying is a cooking method unique to Sichuan cuisine, its principle distinctive feature is that the main ingredients are first slowly stir-fried over a low heat with seasonings, then finished off with supplementary ingredients quickly over a high heat.

1. Thinly cut the beef into matchstick-size shreds. Cut the carrots to the same size.
2. Heat the wok or frying pan over a high heat, add the sesame seed oil, then let it cool a little. Add the beef shreds with 1 tablespoon of the wine or sherry, stir until the shreds are separated, then reduce the heat. Pour off the excess liquid and continue stirring gently until the beef is absolutely dry. Next add the chilli bean paste, Hoi Sin or barbecue sauce, garlic, salt, sugar and the remaining wine or sherry. Stir a few times more.
3. Increase the heat to high, add the carrot shreds, stirring continually; finally add the spring onions, ginger root, Sichuan or black pepper and chilli oil, blend well and serve hot.

Variation:
Use 3 or 4 stalks of celery instead of the carrots (also cut into thin strips); or use both: half carrots and half celery – try it and see!

CLOCKWISE FROM THE TOP: Cantonese beef in Oyster sauce; Beef and green peppers in Cantonese black bean sauce; Sichuan dry-fried shredded beef

蚝油牛肉

CANTONESE BEEF IN OYSTER SAUCE

225-275 g (8-10 oz) beef frying steak
1 teaspoon salt
½ teaspoon freshly ground pepper
1 teaspoon sugar
1 tablespoon light soy sauce
2 tablespoons rice wine or dry sherry
1 tablespoon cornflour
1 egg
1 spring onion, finely chopped
2 slices ginger root, peeled and finely chopped
1 small Chinese cabbage or cos lettuce
4 tablespoons oil
1½ tablespoons Oyster sauce

Preparation time: 15-20 minutes, plus marinating

1. Cut the beef into thin slices about the size of a large postage stamp. Place in a bowl, mix with a pinch of the salt, the pepper, sugar, soy sauce, wine or sherry, cornflour and the egg and marinate for 20-30 minutes.
2. Finely chop the spring onion and ginger root. Wash the Chinese cabbage and cut each leaf into 2 or 3 pieces. If using a cos lettuce, discard the tough outer leaves and tear (do not cut) the larger leaves into 2 or 3 pieces. Leave the small inner leaves whole.
3. Heat 2 tablespoons of the oil in a preheated wok or frying pan, wait for the oil to smoke, then stir-fry the cabbage or lettuce with the remaining salt. Stir constantly until the leaves become limp, 1½-2 minutes for the cabbage but less than 1 minute for the lettuce. Remove quickly and place it on a serving dish.
4. Wash and dry the wok or pan, then heat the remaining oil until very hot. Add the spring onion and ginger root followed by the beef, stirring vigorously, then add the oyster sauce and blend well. Cook for just 1 minute, then serve hot on top of the cabbage or lettuce.

青椒炒鶏絲

SHREDDED CHICKEN BREAST WITH GREEN PEPPERS

1 pair of chicken breasts, boned and skinned
1½ teaspoons salt
1 egg white
3 teaspoons cornflour
225 g (8 oz) green peppers, cored and seeded
1 spring onion, finely chopped
2 slices ginger root, peeled and finely chopped
4 tablespoons oil
2 tablespoons rice wine or dry sherry
1 teaspoon sesame seed oil, to garnish

Preparation time: 20-25 minutes

Take care not to overcook this dish. When correctly done, the chicken should be tender and the peppers crunchy and shining.

1. Remove the white tendon and membrane from the chicken breast meat, then cut the meat into shreds the size of matchsticks. Mix the shreds first with ½ teaspoon of the salt, then the egg white and finally 2 teaspoons of the cornflour.
2. Thinly shred the green pepper to the same size as the chicken. Finely chop the spring onion and ginger root.
3. Warm up the oil in a preheated wok or frying pan, stir-fry the chicken shreds over a moderate heat until their colour changes to white, then remove with a perforated spoon.
4. Increase the heat to high and when the oil is very hot, put in the spring onion and ginger root to flavour the oil. Add the green peppers, stir continuously for about 30 seconds, then add the chicken shreds with the remaining salt and the wine or sherry. Stir for a further ½ minute or so, then add the remaining cornflour mixed with a little water. Blend well, then add the sesame seed oil as a garnish. Serve hot.

> The purpose of marinating chicken breast meat with salt, egg-white and cornflour prior to cooking is a technique known as 'velveting' in English. The coating forms an impenetrable barrier between the meat and the hot oil, thus preserving the natural delicate texture of the chicken breast.
>
> Another point to remember here is that the oil should not be too hot, nor the heat too high when cooking the chicken meat for the first stage. Also, always use fresh as opposed to frozen chicken meat for any of these dishes, as the latter loses a delicacy of flavour and texture.

辣子鶏丁

CHICKEN CUBES WITH WALNUTS SICHUAN STYLE

225 g-275 g (8-10 oz) chicken meat, boned and skinned
½ teaspoon salt
1 egg white
1 tablespoon cornflour
1 green pepper, cored and seeded
50 g (2 oz) walnuts, shelled
4 tablespoons oil
2 spring onions, finely chopped
2 slices ginger root, peeled and finely chopped
Sauce:
1 tablespoon crushed yellow bean sauce
2 teaspoons sugar
2 tablespoons rice wine or dry sherry
1 tablespoon chilli sauce
2 teaspoons cornflour mixed with 1 tablespoon water

Preparation time: 15-20 minutes

1. Cut the chicken meat into small cubes about the size of sugar lumps. Mix with first the salt, then the egg white and finally the cornflour.
2. Cut the green peppers and walnuts to the same size as the chicken cubes.
3. Heat the oil in a preheated wok or frying pan, stir-fry the chicken cubes for 10 seconds, then remove with a perforated spoon.
4. In the same hot oil, add the spring onions, ginger root and walnuts, followed by the yellow bean sauce. Stir a few times, then add the green peppers and chicken cubes. Stir a few times more, then add the sugar, wine or sherry and chilli sauce and cook for 30 seconds. Finally, add the cornflour and water mixture, blend well and serve hot.

Variation:

The walnuts can be replaced by either almonds, cashew nuts or peanuts.

LEFT TO RIGHT: Chicken cubes with walnuts Sichuan style; Shredded chicken breast with green peppers

醬爆鸡脯丁

DICED CHICKEN IN PEKING BEAN SAUCE

1 pair of chicken breasts, boned and skinned
1 egg white
1 tablespoon cornflour mixed with 2 tablespoons water
oil for deep frying
2 tablespoons crushed yellow bean sauce
1 tablespoon sugar
1 tablespoon rice wine or dry sherry
1 teaspoon sesame seed oil

Preparation time: 15-20 minutes

1. Remove the white tendon and membrane from the chicken breast meat, then dice the meat into little cubes.

2. Lightly beat the egg white. Mix the cornflour and water into a smooth paste.

3. Heat the oil in a wok or deep saucepan. Dip the chicken cubes first in the egg white, then in the cornflour and water mixture and drop them into the warm oil (do not let the oil get too hot). Deep fry over a medium heat for a few seconds only, then scoop out with a perforated spoon and drain.

4. Pour off all the oil and replace the wok or pan over a high heat. Put in the crushed yellow bean sauce, stir a few times, add the sugar, stir a few more times, then add the wine or sherry and sesame seed oil, stirring continuously, until the sauce becomes a smooth paste. Add 1 tablespoon of water if necessary. Finally, add the chicken cubes and blend well, until each cube is coated with the sauce. Serve hot.

LEFT TO RIGHT: Mu-shu pork Shandong style; Pork with Sichuan preserved vegetable

椒盐排骨

SICHUAN FRIED PORK SPARE RIBS

450 g (1 lb) pork spare ribs
1 teaspoon salt
1 teaspoon freshly ground Sichuan or black pepper
½ teaspoon five-spice powder
2 tablespoons rice wine or dry sherry
1 egg
2 tablespoons cornflour
oil for deep frying
Dip mixture:
2 teaspoons salt
2 teaspoons ground Sichuan or black pepper

Preparation time: 20-25 minutes, plus marinating

1. Chop each spare rib into 2 or 3 pieces. Place them in a bowl and marinate in the salt, pepper, five-spice powder and wine or sherry for 15 minutes.
2. Beat the egg with the cornflour and make a smooth batter. Mix with the spare ribs.
3. Heat the oil in a wok or deep fryer and deep fry the spare ribs until golden. Scoop out with a perforated spoon, then let the oil get hot again and deep fry the spare ribs once more to crisp them. Serve hot with the salt and pepper mixed together for the dip.

田鍋肉

PORK WITH SICHUAN PRESERVED VEGETABLE

225-275 g (8-10 oz) pork in one piece, not too lean
100 g (4 oz) Sichuan preserved vegetable
100 g (4 oz) leeks, green pepper or broccoli
3 tablespoons oil
2 spring onions, finely chopped
2 slices ginger root, peeled and finely chopped
1 clove garlic, finely chopped
1 tablespoon rice wine or dry sherry
1 tablespoon chilli bean paste
1 teaspoon cornflour mixed with 1 tablespoon water

Preparation time: 15-20 minutes
Cooking time: 25-30 minutes

This is a traditional Sichuan dish that is also known as *Twice-cooked Pork*. It has a fairly hot taste, but if you prefer less hot food, either reduce the amount of Sichuan preserved vegetable by half, or use sweet bean paste instead of chilli bean paste.

1. Place the whole piece of pork in a pan of boiling water and cook for 20-25 minutes. Remove the pork and let it cool a little before cutting it into thin slices about the size of a large postage stamp.
2. Cut the Sichuan preserved vegetable and leeks or other greens into slices about the same size as the pork.
3. Heat the oil in a preheated wok or frying pan and stir-fry the preserved vegetable and greens for about 1 minute, then add the pork, spring onions, ginger root, garlic, wine or sherry and bean paste. Stir for another minute, then add the cornflour and water mixture and blend well together. Serve hot.

The appearance of Sichuan preserved vegetable is somewhat forbidding. It is covered by a thick, red paste that has a strong smell. Before using the preserved vegetable, rinse off the paste in cold water, rubbing the knobby contours to clean them thoroughly, it will become a delightfully crunchy pickled vegetable, with a crispy and refreshing salty aftertaste. Unused knobs should be stored unwashed in an airtight jar, in a cool place or in the refrigerator; it will keep indefinitely.

木樨肉

MU-SHU PORK SHANDONG STYLE

175 g-225 g (6-8 oz) pork steak
10 g (¼ oz) wooden ears
225 g (8 oz) hard white cabbage
2 spring onions
3 eggs
1 teaspoon salt
4 tablespoons oil
1 tablespoon light soy sauce
1 tablespoon rice wine or dry sherry

Preparation time: 20-25 minutes

Mu-shu is the Chinese name for cassia, a fragrant yellow flower that blooms in early autumn. Egg dishes in China are often given the name *Mu-shu* because of the bright yellow colour. Traditionally this dish is eaten as a filling wrapped in thin pancakes (page 76) for a main course, but it can also be served on its own either with rice or as a hot starter.

1. Shred the pork into matchstick-sized segments. Soak the wooden ears in water for about 20 minutes, then rinse and thinly shred them also. Cut the cabbage finely into thin shreds. Cut the spring onions into short lengths.
2. Lightly beat the eggs with a pinch of the salt. Heat 1 tablespoon of the oil in a wok or frying pan and scramble the eggs, until lightly set.
3. Heat the remaining oil and stir-fry the pork shreds for about 30 seconds. Add the cabbage, wooden ears and spring onions, stirring a few times, then add the remaining salt, soy sauce and wine or sherry. Continue stirring for 1-1½ minutes, finally add the scrambled eggs, stirring to break the eggs into shreds also. When all the ingredients are well blended together, it is ready to be served.

Variation:
The cabbage can be substituted with bamboo shoots, celery or bean sprouts (do not use tinned bean sprouts, which will not have the crispness of fresh sprouts; the main characteristic of this very popular vegetable).

慈 爆羊肉

RAPID-FRIED LAMB SLICES

225-275 g (8-10 oz) leg of lamb fillet
about 12 spring onions
4 tablespoons oil
1 tablespoon soy sauce
½ teaspoon salt
1 tablespoon rice wine or dry sherry
½ teaspoon freshly ground Sichuan or black pepper
2 teaspoons cornflour
1 clove garlic, crushed
1 tablespoon sesame seed oil
1 tablespoon vinegar

Preparation time: 15-20 minutes

This dish must be cooked over the highest heat in the shortest possible time, otherwise the meat will not be tender and juicy.

1. Trim off all the fat from the lamb and cut it into slices as thin as possible. Cut the spring onions in half lengthways, then slice them diagonally.
2. Marinate both the meat and spring onions in 1 tablespoon of the oil, the soy sauce, salt, wine or sherry, pepper and cornflour.
3. Heat the remaining oil in a preheated wok or frying pan until smoking, then add first the crushed garlic to flavour the oil, next the lamb and spring onions, stirring constantly over a high heat for a few seconds, and finally the sesame seed oil and vinegar. Blend well, then serve hot.

火爆猪干

FRIED LIVER SICHUAN STYLE

225 g (8 oz) pig's liver
½ teaspoon salt
½ teaspoon freshly ground Sichuan or black pepper
2 tablespoons rice wine or dry sherry
3 teaspoons cornflour
175 g (6 oz) bamboo shoots
4 tablespoons oil
2 spring onions, finely chopped
2 slices ginger root, peeled and finely chopped
1 clove garlic, finely chopped
1½ tablespoons soy sauce
1 teaspoon sugar
1 teaspoon sesame seed oil

Preparation time: 15-20 minutes

1. Cut the liver into slices about the size of a matchbox. Marinate, while preparing the vegetables, in the salt, pepper, 1 tablespoon of the wine or sherry and about 2 teaspoons of the cornflour mixed with a little water.
2. Cut the bamboo shoots into roughly the same size as the liver.
3. Heat the oil in a preheated wok or frying pan until smoking. Add the liver, stir to separate the pieces, then quickly scoop them out with a perforated spoon — literally in and out of the hot oil, otherwise the liver will lose its tenderness.
4. In the same wok or pan, add the spring onions, ginger root and bamboo shoots followed by the liver. Stir a few times, then add the garlic, the remaining wine or sherry, the soy sauce, sugar and sesame seed oil. Finally add the remaining cornflour mixed with a little water and blend well. Serve hot. Do not overcook otherwise the liver will become tough.

Variation:

Instead of bamboo shoots, use wooden ears, soaked for 20 minutes and cut to the same size as the liver, or use a combination of bamboo shoots and wooden ears.

醋溜腰花

STIR-FRIED KIDNEY-FLOWERS SHANDONG STYLE

10 g (¼ oz) wooden ears
50 g (2 oz) bamboo shoots
50 g (2 oz) water chestnuts
100 g (4 oz) seasonal greens (cabbage, broccoli, spinach or lettuce)
1 pair pig's kidneys (about 225 g/8 oz)
1 teaspoon salt
1 tablespoon cornflour
oil for deep frying
1 spring onion, finely chopped
1 slice ginger root, peeled and finely chopped
1 clove garlic, finely chopped
1 tablespoon rice wine or dry sherry
1 tablespoon vinegar
1½ tablespoons soy sauce
1 teaspoon sesame seed oil
3 tablespoons Stock (page 28) or water

Preparation time: 25-30 minutes

This is a most colourful and delicious dish. People who do not normally like the taste of kidneys just cannot help falling for this recipe.

1. Soak the wooden ears in water for 15-20 minutes, then rinse and discard any hard parts. Cut the bamboo shoots and water chestnuts into small slices. Blanch the green vegetable.
2. Split each kidney in half lengthways and discard the white and dark parts in the middle. Score the surface of each half kidney diagonally in a criss-cross pattern, then cut each half into 6-8 pieces. Mix with ½ teaspoon of the salt and about ½ tablespoon of the cornflour.
3. Heat the oil in a wok or deep saucepan. While it is heating, quickly blanch the kidney pieces in a pan of boiling water, strain and pat dry with a clean cloth or kitchen paper. Deep-fry the kidney pieces in hot oil for a few seconds only, then scoop out with a perforated spoon.
4. Pour off most of the oil, leaving about 1 tablespoon in the wok or pan. Add the spring onion, ginger root and garlic, stirring a few times. Next add the wooden ears, bamboo shoots, water chestnuts, kidneys, the remaining salt, the wine or sherry, vinegar, soy sauce and sesame seed oil, stirring constantly for about 1 minute. Finally add the remaining cornflour mixed with the stock or water and blend well. Serve hot.

LEFT TO RIGHT: Stir-fried kidney-flowers Shandong style;
Rapid-fried lamb slices

芙蓉鸡

CHICKEN BREAST AND EGG WHITE

1 pair of chicken breasts, boned and skinned
1½ teaspoons salt
2 egg whites
1 tablespoon cornflour
4 tablespoons oil
1 lettuce heart
1 slice ginger root, peeled and finely chopped
1 spring onion, finely chopped
100 g (4 oz) green peas
1 tablespoon rice wine or dry sherry
1 teaspoon sesame seed oil

Preparation time: 10-15 minutes

1. Remove the white tendon and membrane from the chicken meat, then cut it into thin slices about the size of a large postage stamp. Mix the chicken slices with first ½ teaspoon of the salt, then the egg white and finally the cornflour.
2. Warm up the oil in a preheated wok or frying pan, stir-fry the chicken slices over a moderate heat for about 30 seconds or until their colour turns white, remove with a perforated spoon.
3. Increase the heat to high, add the lettuce leaves and stir-fry with another ½ teaspoon of the salt until limp, remove and place on a serving dish.
4. Add the ginger root and spring onion to the wok or pan, followed by the chicken slices and green peas, then add the remaining salt, wine or sherry, stir and blend well. Finally add the sesame seed oil and serve hot on top of the lettuce leaves.

西芹鸡丁

CHICKEN CUBES WITH CELERY

1 pair of chicken breasts, skinned and boned
½ teaspoon salt
1 egg white
1 tablespoon cornflour
1 small head celery
4 tablespoons oil
1 tablespoon rice wine or dry sherry
1 tablespoon light soy sauce

Preparation time: 15-20 minutes

SHREDDED PORK IN PEKING BEAN SAUCE

450 g (1 lb) leg of pork, boned but not skinned
450 ml (¾ pint) Stock (page 28)
½ teaspoon salt
1 tablespoon crushed yellow bean sauce
2 tablespoons rice wine or dry sherry
2 tablespoons plain flour
1 small green pepper, cored and seeded
oil for deep frying
1 teaspoon sugar
1 tablespoon soy sauce

Preparation time: 10-15 minutes
Cooking time: about 40 minutes

1. Place the pork in a saucepan with the stock, bring to the boil, then cover and simmer for 25-30 minutes.
2. Take the meat out, remove the skin, then cut the meat into strips about the size of potato chips. Marinate in the salt, yellow bean sauce, wine or sherry and flour.
3. Cut the green pepper into strips the same size as the pork.
4. Heat the oil in a wok or deep saucepan until very hot, fry the pork strips until golden, scoop out and drain.
5. Pour off the oil and return the pork to the same wok or pan. Add the sugar, soy sauce and green pepper, stirring a few times over a high heat. Blend well and serve hot.

1. Remove the white tendon and membrane from the chicken, then dice it into small cubes about the size of sugar lumps. Mix with first the salt, then the egg white and finally about ½ tablespoon of the cornflour.
2. Cut the celery sticks into small chunks diagonally, roughly the same size as the chicken cubes.
3. Warm the oil in a preheated wok or frying pan, stir-fry the chicken cubes over a moderate heat for 30 seconds or until their colour turns to white, then scoop them out with a perforated spoon.
4. Increase the heat and when the oil is very hot, stir-fry the celery for about 1 minute, then add the chicken with the wine or sherry and soy sauce and cook for a further minute at the very most. Finally, add the remaining cornflour mixed with a little water, blend well and serve hot. The chicken should be tender and the celery crisp and crunchy.

炸肉丸子

SHANGHAI CRISPY MEATBALLS

450 g (1 lb) pork, not too lean
1 teaspoon salt
2 tablespoons light soy sauce
1 tablespoon rice wine or dry sherry
1 teaspoon sugar
1 egg
2 teaspoons freshly ground Sichuan or black pepper
1 teaspoon peeled and finely chopped ginger root
1 teaspoon finely chopped spring onion
about 3 tablespoons cornflour
oil for deep frying

Preparation time: 40-45 minutes

1. Finely chop the pork, mix with the salt, soy sauce, wine or sherry, sugar, egg, pepper, ginger root, spring onions and 2 tablespoons of the cornflour. Stir for 2-3 minutes until everything is well blended and slightly thickened.
2. Make this mixture into about 2 dozen small meatballs and coat each ball with a little more cornflour.
3. Heat up the oil in a wok or deep fryer until bubbling, then reduce the heat to moderate, deep fry the meatballs a few at a time, until golden. Scoop out with a perforated spoon and drain.
4. Heat up the oil again and return the meatballs for a few seconds to crispen them just before serving.

FROM THE LEFT: Shredded pork in Peking bean sauce; Chicken cubes with celery; Chicken breast and egg white

鴛鴦虾仁

RED AND WHITE PRAWNS WITH GREEN VEGETABLE

2 teaspoons salt
450 g (1 lb) peeled raw prawns
1 egg white
1 tablespoon cornflour
225 g (8 oz) mange-tout peas or broccoli
600 ml (1 pint) oil
2 spring onions, finely chopped
2 slices ginger root, peeled and finely chopped
2 tablespoons rice wine or dry sherry
1 tablespoon tomato purée
1 tablespoon chilli sauce

Preparation time: 25-30 minutes

This is a very colourful dish for a special occasion. Served as a starter, it is sufficient for 8-10 people, otherwise it will serve 4-6 in conjunction with 1 or 2 other dishes. A purchased Sichuan Chilli and Tomato sauce, which is mild as it contains sugar, can be used instead of the tomato purée and chilli sauce.
The Chinese name for this dish is 'Yuanyang Prawns' or 'Mandarin Ducks Prawns'. Mandarin ducks are also known as 'love birds' because they are always seen lovingly together, therefore they are often used as symbols of affection and happiness. In China, pillows and bed covers embroidered with mandarin ducks are given as wedding presents.

1. Mix a pinch of the salt with the prawns in a bowl. Add the egg white, then the cornflour.
2. Top and tail the peas or cut the broccoli into small florets and dice the stalks.
3. Heat about 3 tablespoons of the oil in a preheated wok or frying pan and stir-fry the green vegetable with about 1 teaspoon of the salt (the mange-toute peas will only take 1½-2 minutes, broccoli will take about 1 minute longer). Remove and place the vegetable in the centre of a serving platter.
4. Wash and dry the wok or pan, heat the remaining oil until hot, stir-fry the prawns for 1 minute at the most. Remove and drain.
5. Pour off most of the oil, leaving about 1 tablespoon in the wok or pan, add the spring onions and ginger root, followed by the prawns. Add the remaining salt and wine or sherry, stir a few times, then remove half of the prawns and place them at one end of the platter.
6. Now add the tomato purée and chilli sauce to the prawns in the wok or pan, stir a few seconds to blend the sauce, then remove and place the prawns at the other end of the platter. Serve hot.

糖醋大虾

CANTONESE SWEET AND SOUR PRAWNS

225 g (8 oz) Pacific or king prawns
1 egg white
1 tablespoon cornflour
oil for deep frying
1 spring onion, finely chopped
2 slices ginger root, peeled and finely chopped
Sauce:
2 tablespoons sugar
1 tablespoon rice wine or dry sherry
1 tablespoon soy sauce
1 tablespoon vinegar
2 teaspoons cornflour mixed with 2 tablespoons Stock (page 28) or water

Preparation time: 10-15 minutes

Like *Rapid fried prawns in shells* (page 14), this dish is best eaten with chopsticks or fingers, though it should be served hot rather than cold.

1. Trim the heads, whiskers and legs off the prawns but leave on the shells. Cut each prawn into 2 or 3 pieces. Mix the egg white with the cornflour and coat the prawns with this mixture.
2. Heat the oil in a wok or deep saucepan but before it gets too hot, add the prawns, piece by piece and fry until golden, then remove with a perforated spoon and drain.
3. Pour off most of the oil, leaving about 1 tablespoon in the wok or pan and stir-fry the spring onion and ginger root, then add the sugar, wine or sherry, soy sauce and vinegar, stirring constantly. When the sugar has dissolved, add the prawns and blend well, then add the cornflour mixed with the stock or water. Stir constantly and serve as soon as the sauce thickens.

TOP TO BOTTOM: Cantonese sweet and sour prawns; Red and white prawns with green vegetable

炸蟹丸子

DEEP-FRIED CRAB MEAT BALLS

450 g (1 lb) crab meat
50 g (2 oz) pork fat
4-6 water chestnuts, peeled
1 egg
1 tablespoon rice wine or dry sherry
1 teaspoon salt
1 teaspoon finely chopped and peeled ginger root
1 teaspoon finely chopped spring onion
2 tablespoons cornflour
oil for deep frying
1 lettuce heart, to serve

Preparation time: about 30 minutes

Either fresh, frozen or even canned crabmeat can be used for this recipe. Also prawns or a mixture of crabmeat and prawns can be substituted.

1. Finely chop the crab meat, pork fat and water chestnuts. Mix in a bowl together with the egg, wine or sherry, salt, ginger root, spring onion and cornflour.
2. Chill the mixture for 1 hour to harden. (This is not necessary in winter or if your kitchen is cool.) Then make into approximately 24 small balls about the size of walnuts.
3. Heat the oil in a wok or deep fryer until hot, then reduce the heat to moderate. Gently lower the balls into the oil one by one and deep fry them until light golden.
4. Scoop out with a perforated spoon and increase the heat to high, then put the balls back in the oil for a few seconds, until they are golden brown. Serve hot on a bed of lettuce leaves.

Variation:
The crab meat balls can be made and cooked as far as step 3 the day before, then warmed up when required as step 4. Alternatively, they can be served 'wet' by placing them in 120 ml (4 fl oz) stock in a wok or pan, bringing them to a boil and simmering gently for 5 minutes, thickening the gravy with 2 teaspoons cornflour mixed with a little water or stock. Garnish with 1 tablespoon finely chopped ham.

炸 鳳 尾 虾

PHOENIX-TAIL PRAWNS

225 g (8 oz) Pacific or king prawns
½ teaspoon salt
2 tablespoons rice wine or dry sherry
1 spring onion, finely chopped
2 slices ginger root, peeled and finely chopped
oil for deep frying
3 egg whites
1 tablespoon cornflour
3 tablespoons plain flour
4 tablespoons breadcrumbs
1 tablespoon salt
1 tablespoon freshly ground Sichuan or black pepper
1 lettuce, to serve

Preparation time: 35-45 minutes

These prawns are deep-fried with their tails still attached, which is decorative and makes them easy to handle.

1. Wash and shell the prawns but leave the tail pieces firmly attached. Split the prawns in half lengthways and discard the black intestinal vein.
2. Dry the prawns thoroughly with kitchen paper and mix them with the salt, wine or sherry, spring onion and ginger root, together with 1 teaspoon of the oil.
3. Put the remainder of the oil in a wok or deep fryer and while waiting for it to heat up, beat the egg whites in a bowl until frothy, then fold in the cornflour.
4. When the oil is hot, reduce the heat for a while, coat the prawns in the plain flour, then dip each piece in the egg white mixture and lastly roll them in breadcrumbs. Lower them into the oil one by one and fry in batches until golden, then remove and drain.
5. To make the salt and pepper dip, mix equal portions of the salt and pepper and heat for 2-3 minutes in a preheated dry frying pan over a low heat.
6. Place the prawns on a bed of lettuce leaves and serve with the salt and pepper dip.

三 鮮 海 味

THREE SEA-FLAVOURS (SCALLOPS, PRAWNS AND SQUID)

100 g (4 oz) squid
100 g (4 oz) Pacific or king prawns
4 scallops
1 teaspoon salt
½ teaspoon freshly ground pepper
1 medium red pepper, cored and seeded
3 stalks celery
1 carrot
2 slices ginger root, peeled
2 spring onions
150 ml (¼ pint) oil
1 tablespoon rice wine or dry sherry
1 tablespoon soy sauce
½-1 tablespoon hot chilli bean sauce
2 teaspoons cornflour mixed with 2 tablespoons Stock (page 28) or water
1 teaspoon sesame seed oil, to garnish

Preparation time: 30-35 minutes

This is a colourful and delicious dish. It epitomizes the harmonious contrast of Chinese cooking.

1. Prepare the squid as in the recipe for *Stir-fried squid flowers* (page 50). Shell the prawns and cut each into 2 or 3 pieces. Cut the scallops into quarters. Mix the scallops, squid and prawns with the salt and pepper.
2. Cut the red pepper, celery and carrot into pieces roughly the same shape and size as an oblong postage stamp. Finely shred the ginger root and spring onions.
3. Heat the oil in a preheated wok or frying pan, stir-fry the scallops, prawns and squid for about 1 minute, then remove with a perforated spoon and drain.
4. Pour off most of the oil, leaving about 1 tablespoon, then add the ginger root and spring onions, followed by the red pepper, celery and carrot. Stir for about 1 minute, then return the 3 sea-flavours to the wok or pan, add the wine or sherry, soy sauce and hot chilli bean sauce. Stir a few more times, then add the cornflour mixed with stock or water and blend well. As soon as the gravy starts to thicken, garnish with sesame seed oil and serve hot.

CLOCKWISE FROM THE LEFT: Fish slices with wine sauce; Three sea flavours; Phoenix-tail prawns

糟 熘 魚 片

FISH SLICES WITH WINE SAUCE

450 g (1 lb) plaice or sole fillet
1 egg white
2 tablespoons cornflour mixed with 5 tablespoons water
oil for deep frying
1½ teaspoons salt
1 teaspoon sugar
300 ml (½ pint) Stock (page 28)
4 tablespoons rice wine or dry sherry
1 teaspoon sesame seed oil, to garnish

Preparation time: 10-15 minutes

The oil for deep frying must be fresh or it will colour
the fish.

1. Cut the fish into large pieces, leaving the skin on.
Mix them first with the egg white and then in the
cornflour and water mixture.
2. Heat the oil in a wok or deep saucepan, but before it
becomes too hot, add the fish pieces one by one, reserving the leftover cornflour mixture, and fry over a
medium heat for 1 minute, using a pair of chopsticks to
separate each slice. Scoop them out with a perforated
spoon and drain.
3. Pour off the oil, return the fish slices to the wok or
pan, then add the salt, sugar, stock and wine or sherry.
Bring the sauce to the boil, reduce the heat and simmer
for 2 minutes.
4. Add the remaining cornflour and water mixture
very slowly to the wok or pan, increase the heat to high
and tilt the wok to distribute the cornflour and water
mixture evenly over the fish slices.
5. As soon as the gravy thickens, garnish with sesame
seed oil and serve hot.

油 爆 魷 魚
STIR-FRIED SQUID FLOWERS

---

450 g (1 lb) squid
1 slice ginger root, peeled and finely chopped
1 spring onion, finely chopped
3 tablespoons oil
1 tablespoon rice wine or dry sherry
1 teaspoon salt
1 tablespoon soy sauce
1 teaspoon sugar
fresh coriander leaves, to garnish

Preparation time: about 20-25 minutes

1. Clean the squid, discarding the head and transparent backbone as well as the ink bag. Peel off the thin skin and make a criss-cross pattern on the *inside*, then cut into pieces about the size of an oblong postage stamp, so that when they are cooked they will open up and resemble ears of corn – hence the name of this dish.
2. Heat the oil in a preheated wok or frying pan, add the ginger root and spring onion, followed by the squid. Stir-fry for about 30 seconds. Add the wine or sherry, salt, soy sauce and sugar and continue stirring for 2 minutes at the most. Do not overcook otherwise the squid will become tough.
3. Serve hot, garnished with fresh coriander leaves, which should not be too finely chopped.

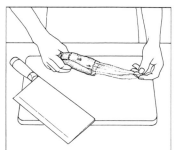
Remove the transparent backbone and ink bag.

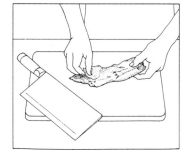
Peel off the thin skin.

Open out and clean the inside.

Score the inside in a criss-cross pattern.

TOP TO BOTTOM: Stir-fried squid flowers; Sichuan prawns in chilli and tomato sauce; Shredded fish with celery

干 烧 明 虾

SICHUAN PRAWNS IN CHILLI AND TOMATO SAUCE

1 teaspoon salt
225 g (8 oz) peeled raw prawns
1 egg white
2 teaspoons cornflour
oil for deep frying
1 spring onion, finely chopped
2 slices ginger root, peeled and finely chopped
1 clove garlic, finely chopped
1 tablespoon rice wine or dry sherry
1 tablespoon tomato purée
1 tablespoon chilli sauce
1 lettuce heart

Preparation time: 20-25 minutes

1. Mix a pinch of the salt with the prawns, add the egg white, then the cornflour.
2. Warm up the oil in a wok or deep saucepan, add the prawns, stirring to separate, and deep-fry for about 30 seconds over a medium heat. Remove and drain.
3. Pour off most of the oil, leaving about 1 tablespoon in the wok or pan, turn the heat up to high, add the spring onion, ginger root and garlic to flavour the oil, then add the prawns and stir a few times.
4. Add the remaining salt, wine or sherry, tomato purée and chilli sauce, stirring continually. When all the sauces are well blended, remove and serve on a bed of lettuce leaves.

酱 汁 鱼 块

BRAISED FISH STEAK

450 g (1 lb) fish cutlets (cod or haddock)
flour, for dusting
300 ml (½ pint) oil
2 slices ginger root, peeled and finely chopped
2 spring onions, finely chopped
2 tablespoons rice wine or dry sherry
1 tablespoon sugar
1 teaspoon salt
1 tablespoon vinegar
5 tablespoons Stock (page 28)
1 tablespoon cornflour mixed with a little water
1 teaspoon sesame seed oil, to garnish

Preparation time: about 15 minutes

鱼 丝 芹 菜

SHREDDED FISH WITH CELERY

225 g (8 oz) fish fillet (cod or haddock)
1 teaspoon salt
1 tablespoon rice wine or dry sherry
1 egg white
1 tablespoon cornflour
1 celery heart
oil for deep frying
25 g (1 oz) cooked ham, thinly shredded, to garnish

Preparation time: 20-25 minutes

1. Remove the skin from the fish fillet and cut the fish into thin shreds. Place in a bowl and sprinkle with a pinch of the salt, then add first the wine or sherry, next the egg white and then the cornflour. Leave the fish to marinate while preparing and cooking the celery.
2. Cut the celery heart into thin shreds.
3. Heat about 2 tablespoons of the oil in a preheated wok or frying pan, then stir-fry the celery, with the remaining salt for about 1½ minutes. Place it on a serving dish.
4. Heat the remaining oil in a wok or deep fryer, reduce the heat to medium and deep fry the fish shreds for about 2 minutes, separating them with a pair of chopsticks. When all the shreds are floating on the surface of the oil, scoop them out with a perforated spoon and drain, then place them on top of the celery.
5. Garnish with the cooked ham and serve either hot or cold.

Try to use the small cutlets from the tail end of the fish.

1. Leave the skin on the cutlets and lightly dust each one with flour.
2. Heat the oil in a preheated wok or frying pan, fry the fish pieces for about 1 minute over a high heat, then remove with a perforated spoon and drain.
3. Pour off any excess oil, leaving about 1 tablespoon in the wok or pan, add the ginger root, spring onions, wine or sherry, sugar, salt, vinegar and stock, together with the fish pieces.
4. Reduce the heat and simmer gently for 2 minutes. Add the cornflour and water mixture. Increase the heat and when the gravy thickens, garnish with sesame seed oil and serve hot.

魚 香 茄 子

AUBERGINE WITH SICHUAN 'FISH SAUCE'

4-6 dried red chillis
450 g (1 lb) aubergines
oil for deep frying
3-4 spring onions, finely chopped
1 slice ginger root, peeled and finely chopped
1 clove garlic, finely chopped
1 teaspoon sugar
1 tablespoon soy sauce
1 tablespoon vinegar
1 tablespoon chilli bean paste
2 teaspoons cornflour mixed with 2 tablespoons water
1 teaspoon sesame seed oil, to garnish

Preparation time: 20-25 minutes

The interesting point is that no fish is used in this recipe – the sauce is normally used for cooking a fish dish, hence the name 'fish sauce'.

1. Soak the dried red chillis for 5-10 minutes, then cut them into small pieces discarding the stalks (or leave them whole if small). Peel the aubergines and discard the stalks, then cut them into diamond-shaped chunks.
2. Heat the oil in a wok or deep saucepan and deep fry the aubergines for about 1½-2 minutes or until soft. Scoop out with a perforated spoon and drain.
3. Pour off the oil and return the aubergines to the wok or pan. Add the red chillis, spring onions, ginger root and garlic, stir a few times, then add the sugar, soy sauce, vinegar and chilli bean paste and continue stirring for about 1 minute. Finally add the cornflour and water mixture, blend well and garnish with the sesame seed oil. Serve either hot or cold.

Variation:
100 g (4 oz) thinly shredded pork can be used in addition to the various ingredients to make the 'fish sauce'. In which case, add the pork at the beginning of step 3 just before you return the deep-fried aubergines to the wok or pan.

TOP TO BOTTOM: Stir-fried spinach and bean curd; Aubergine with Sichuan 'fish sauce'; Braised broccoli; Stir-fried mixed vegetables

菠菜炒豆腐

STIR-FRIED SPINACH AND BEAN CURD

225 g (8 oz) spinach
2 cakes bean curd
4 tablespoons oil
1 teaspoon salt
1 teaspoon sugar
1 tablespoon soy sauce
1 teaspoon sesame seed oil

Preparation time: 10 minutes

1. Wash the spinach well, shaking off the excess water.
2. Cut up each cake of bean curd into about 8 pieces.
3. Heat the oil in a wok or frying pan, fry the bean curd pieces until they are golden, turning them over once or twice gently. Remove with a perforated spoon and set aside.
4. Stir-fry the spinach in the remaining oil for about 30 seconds or until the leaves are limp. Add the bean curd pieces, salt, sugar and soy sauce, blend well and cook together for another 1-1½ minutes. Add the sesame seed oil and serve hot.

油燜西芝

BRAISED BROCCOLI

450 g (1 lb) broccoli or cauliflower
3 tablespoons oil
1 teaspoon salt
1 teaspoon sugar
3 tablespoons Stock (page 28) or water

Preparation time: 10 minutes

1. Cut the broccoli or cauliflower into florets, do not discard the stalks but peel off the tough skin.
2. Heat the oil in a preheated wok or frying pan and stir-fry the broccoli or cauliflower for about 30 seconds. Add the salt, sugar and stock or water and cook for 2-3 minutes at most, stirring a few times during cooking. Serve hot.

炒鮮蔬

STIR-FRIED MIXED VEGETABLES

100 g (4 oz) fresh bean sprouts
100 g (4 oz) bamboo shoots
100 g (4 oz) mange-tout peas or broccoli
100 g (4 oz) carrots
3 tablespoons oil
1 teaspoon salt
1 teaspoon sugar
1 tablespoon Stock (page 28) or water

Preparation time: 15-20 minutes

Do not use tinned bean sprouts; if fresh sprouts are not available, thinly shred 2 sticks of celery instead. Similarly, the bamboo shoots can be replaced by either cabbage, courgettes or cauliflower. The main idea of this recipe is to give the dish a harmonious contrast in colour and texture.

1. Wash the fresh bean sprouts in cold water, discard the husks and other bits and pieces that float to the surface. It is not necessary to top and tail each sprout.
2. Cut the bamboo shoots, broccoli and carrots into thin slices. If using mange-tout peas they only need to be topped and tailed.
3. Heat the oil in a preheated wok or frying pan. Put in the bamboo shoots, mange-tout peas or broccoli and carrots, stir for about 1 minute, then add the bean sprouts with the salt and sugar. Stir for another minute or so, then add some stock or water if necessary. Do not overcook otherwise the vegetables will lose their crunchiness. Serve hot.

When stir-frying, choose the freshest vegetables you can find: do not leave them lying around too long before use and always wash vegetables *before* cutting them up in order to avoid losing vitamins in water.

Cook vegetables as soon as you have cut them, so that not too much of the vitamin content is destroyed by exposure to the air.

Never overcook the vegetables, nor use too much water in cooking. Avoid using a lid over the wok or pan unless specified, as it will spoil the brightness of the colour.

BRAISED & STEAMED DISHES

鍋燒牛肉

BRAISED BEEF

750 g (1½-1¾ lb) shin of beef
2 tablespoons rice wine or dry sherry
2 tablespoons soy sauce
1 teaspoon five-spice powder
2 slices ginger root
225 g (8 oz) tomatoes, halved or quartered
50 g (2 oz) crystallized brown sugar
225 g (8 oz) carrots, peeled
1 teaspoon salt

Preparation time: 20 minutes
Cooking time: about 2 hours

1. Cut the beef into 4 cm (1½ inch) cubes and trim off any excess fat, but leave the sinew in the meat as it will give the liquid extra flavour and richness.
2. Place the meat in a saucepan with enough water to cover, add the wine or sherry, soy sauce, five-spice powder, ginger root and tomatoes. Bring to the boil, then reduce the heat, cover and simmer for 45 minutes. Now add the brown sugar and cook for a further 30 minutes.
3. Cut the carrots to the same size as the beef. Add them with the salt to the beef and cook for a further 30 minutes until the liquid has reduced and thickened into a delicious sauce, increasing the heat if necessary. Serve hot.

Variation:
Shin is one of the most economical cuts of beef obtainable; another cheap cut that is suitable for this recipe is brisket of beef. Should you decide to use a more expensive cut such as braising steak, then reduce the cooking time by at least 30-45 minutes.

Any left-overs can be warmed up and served again; in fact this dish always tastes even better when reheated, as it gives you the chance to remove any excess fat once it has cooled.

粉蒸牛肉

STEAMED BEEF SICHUAN STYLE

750 g (1½-1¾ lb) beef (topside)
1 teaspoon salt
2 tablespoons rice wine or dry sherry
1 tablespoon soy sauce
2 tablespoons chilli bean paste
1 teaspoon sugar
3 slices ginger root, peeled and finely chopped
4 spring onions, finely chopped
freshly ground Sichuan or black pepper
1 tablespoon oil
75 g (3 oz) ground rice
1 lettuce or cabbage
To garnish:
1 teaspoon sesame seed oil
finely chopped spring onion

Preparation time: about 30 minutes
Cooking time: 15 minutes

1. Cut the beef into matchbox-sized thin slices, marinate in the salt, wine or sherry, soy sauce, chilli bean paste, sugar, ginger root, spring onions, pepper and oil. Leave to marinade for 20 minutes.
2. Meanwhile, roast the ground rice in a dry frying pan, until it is aromatic and golden brown. Line the bottom of a steamer with lettuce or cabbage leaves, then coat each slice of beef with ground rice and arrange in neat layers on top.
3. Steam vigorously for 15 minutes. Garnish with sesame seed oil and more finely chopped spring onion. Serve hot; and if you like your food really spicy, serve the beef with chilli sauce as a dip!

Braised beef; Steamed beef Sichuan style

金华玉樹鷄

CANTONESE CHICKEN, HAM AND GREENS

1 × 1¼ kg (2½-2¾ lb) fresh young chicken
2 slices ginger root
2 spring onions
2 teaspoons salt
225 g (8 oz) cooked ham
225 g (8 oz) broccoli or lettuce heart
3 tablespoons oil
1 tablespoon cornflour
50 ml (2 fl oz) Stock (page 28) or cooking liquor

Preparation time: 25-30 minutes
Cooking time: about 1½ hours

This dish can either be served cold as a starter or part of a buffet-type meal; or served hot as a main course for a big dinner. When served on its own together with, say, rice or noodles, it is ample for 4-6 people.

1. Clean the chicken well, place it in a saucepan and cover with cold water. Add the ginger root, spring onions and 1½ teaspoons of the salt. Bring to the boil, then cover and simmer gently for 25-30 minutes. Turn off the heat but keep the pan covered and leave the bird to cook in the hot water for at least 1 hour. Do not be tempted to lift the lid for a peep – the heat will escape and the chicken will not be cooked properly.
2. Heat 2 tablespoons of the oil in a wok or frying pan and stir-fry the broccoli or lettuce with a little salt, or part-boil them in the cooking liquor from the chicken. Drain and arrange them around the edge of the dish.
3. To serve, remove the chicken, gently pull the meat off the bone (with the skin), then cut into small slices. Cut the ham into thin slices of the same size.
4. Arrange the chicken and ham slices in alternate layers in the middle of the serving dish.
5. To make the sauce, heat the remaining oil in a clean wok or saucepan. Combine the cornflour and stock (or cooking liquor from the chicken) and pour into the pan. Add the remaining salt and stir over a moderate heat until thickened, then pour evenly over the chicken and ham, to form a thin coat of transparent jelly.

红 烧 鸡 块

SHANGHAI BRAISED CHICKEN

1 × 1½ kg (3-3½ lb) young chicken
2 slices ginger root, peeled
2 spring onions
2 tablespoons oil
2 tablespoons rice wine or dry sherry
3 tablespoons soy sauce
1 tablespoon sugar
150 ml (¼ pint) water or Stock (page 28)
4-5 Chinese dried mushrooms
225 g (8 oz) bamboo shoots, sliced

Preparation time: 20-25 minutes
Cooking time: about 45 minutes

Four chicken pieces can be used instead but make sure you get an assortment of legs, breasts and wings rather than just one kind. Cut them into 12-14 pieces.

1. If using a whole chicken, cut it into 12-14 pieces. Cut the ginger root and spring onions into small pieces.
2. Heat the oil in a wok or saucepan, put in the ginger root and spring onions, followed by the chicken pieces and fry for about 5 minutes, until lightly browned. Add the wine or sherry, soy sauce and sugar, together with the water or stock. Reduce the heat and cook gently for 20 to 25 minutes, stirring from time to time.
3. Meanwhile, soak the mushrooms in warm water for about 20 minutes, then squeeze dry and discard the hard stalks. Add the mushrooms to the chicken, together with the slices of bamboo shoots. Increase the heat to high and cook for a further 10 minutes or until the liquid has almost all evaporated. Serve hot.

Variation:
Use carrots instead of bamboo shoots; and the Chinese dried mushrooms can be replaced by fresh mushrooms.

烩 鸡 翅

CHICKEN WINGS ASSEMBLY

12 chicken wings
¼ teaspoon salt
1 tablespoon sugar
2 tablespoons soy sauce
2 tablespoons rice wine or dry sherry
1 tablespoon cornflour
2 tablespoons oil
1 clove garlic, crushed
3 spring onions, cut into short lengths
3-4 tablespoons Stock (page 28) or water
1 teaspoon sesame seed oil, to garnish (optional)

Preparation time: 10-15 minutes
Cooking time: 25-30 minutes

1. Trim off and discard the tip of the wings (they can be used for stock), and cut the remainder of the wings into 2 pieces by breaking at the joint. Mix them with the salt, sugar, soy sauce, wine or sherry and cornflour. Marinate for about 10 minutes, turning them once or twice.
2. Heat the oil in a preheated wok or frying pan. Stir-fry the chicken wings for about 1 minute, or until they start to turn brown, then scoop them out with a perforated spoon. Add the crushed garlic and spring onions to the wok or pan to flavour the oil, then add the chicken wings and a little of the stock or water. Stir, then cover and cook over a fairly high heat for about 5 minutes, listen carefully for the sizzling noise to make sure it is not burning. Add a little more stock or water if necessary and stir gently to make sure that the chicken pieces are not stuck to the bottom of the pan or wok.
3. Cover and cook for a further 5-10 minutes, until the sauce is almost entirely absorbed, then add the sesame seed oil as a garnish if desired, stir a few times to blend well and serve hot.

Using a sharp knife, cut off the tip of each chicken wing.

Cut between the joint on the remaining wing to produce 2 pieces.

CLOCKWISE FROM THE BOTTOM: Chicken wings assembly; Shanghai braised chicken; Cantonese chicken, ham and greens

香酥鴨

AROMATIC AND CRISPY SICHUAN DUCK

1 × 1½ kg (3-3½ lb) duckling
2 teaspoons salt
4 slices ginger root
3 spring onions
3 tablespoons rice wine or dry sherry
1 teaspoon five-spice powder
4 star anise
2 teaspoons Sichuan or black peppercorns
oil for deep frying
To serve:
12 Thin pancakes (page 76)
4 tablespoons Hoi Sin or barbecue sauce
6 spring onions, cut into thin strips

Preparation time: about 1 hour, plus overnight marinating
Cooking time: 2¾ hours

This dish is claimed to be the forerunner of the world-renowned Peking Duck. Whatever is the truth, it is on the menu in most Peking-style restaurants, and it is eaten exactly like the Peking duck, that is, wrapped in pancakes together with strips of spring onion and Hoi Sin sauce.

1. Clean the duck well, split it down the back and rub it with salt on both sides. Marinate in a deep dish with the ginger root, spring onions, wine or sherry, five-spice powder, star anise and peppercorns overnight or for at least 3 hours, turning over the duck several times.
2. Place the duck with the marinade in the deep dish in a steamer and steam vigorously for at least 2½ hours. Remove and discard the marinated vegetables.
3. Heat up the oil in a wok or deep-fryer, then deep-fry the duck for 10-12 minutes over a medium heat until brown and crispy, remove and drain.
4. To serve, pull the meat off the bone and wrap it in the pancakes with strips of spring onions and Hoi Sin or barbecue sauce.

Variation:
If you do not have a steamer large enough to hold a whole duck, after marinating in a large bowl, it can be transferred to a saucepan and cooked with 1½ litres (2½ pints) stock. Simmer gently for 2½-3 hours, then lift the duck out of the pan to drain and cool a little before deep frying.

清蒸滑鸡

STEAMED CHICKEN WITH MUSHROOMS

---

750 g (1½-1¾ lb) chicken meat
1 teaspoon salt
1 teaspoon sugar
1 tablespoon rice wine or dry sherry
1 teaspoon cornflour
3-4 Chinese dried mushrooms
2 slices ginger root, peeled
1 teaspoon oil
freshly ground Sichuan or black pepper
1 teaspoon sesame seed oil

**Preparation time: 10-15 minutes, plus soaking
Cooking time: 20 minutes**

This dish is best using the breasts and thighs of a young chicken.

1. Cut the chicken into bite-sized pieces and mix with the salt, sugar, wine or sherry and cornflour. Soak the mushrooms in warm water for about 20 minutes, then squeeze dry and discard the hard stalks.
2. Thinly shred the mushrooms and ginger root. Grease a heatproof plate or dish with the oil.
3. Place the chicken pieces on the plate with the mushrooms and ginger root shreds on top, then add the ground pepper and sesame seed oil.
4. Place the chicken dish in a steamer and steam vigorously for 20 minutes. Serve hot.

八宝鸭

EIGHT-TREASURE DUCK

---

1 × 2 kg (4½-4¾ lb) duckling
2 tablespoons dark soy sauce
Stuffing:
150 g (5 oz) glutinous rice
200 ml (⅓ pint) water
4-5 Chinese dried mushrooms
1 tablespoon dried shrimps
1 duck gizzard (optional)
100 g (4 oz) bamboo shoots
100 g (4 oz) cooked ham
2 tablespoons oil
2 spring onions, finely chopped
2 slices ginger root, peeled and finely chopped
½ teaspoon salt
1 tablespoon soy sauce
2 tablespoons rice wine or dry sherry
finely chopped spring onions, to garnish

**Preparation time: 35-40 minutes
Cooking time: 1¼ hours
Oven: 200°C, 400°F, Gas Mark 6;
     180°C, 350°F, Gas Mark 4**

The name of this dish refers to the various ingredients used for the stuffing. If glutinous rice is unavailable, use round pudding rice instead. If possible reserve the duck's gizzard for the stuffing.

1. Clean the duck well both inside and out, pat dry with paper towels, then brush the skin with the dark soy sauce.
2. Cook the glutinous rice in the water (page 79).
3. Soak the dried mushrooms in the warm water for 20 minutes, squeeze dry and discard the hard stalks, then cut each mushroom into small cubes. Soak the shrimps also in warm water for 20 minutes. Boil the gizzard (if using) gently in water for 10-15 minutes, then cut it into small cubes also. Cut the bamboo shoots and ham to the same size.
4. Heat the oil in a preheated wok or frying pan, put in the spring onions and ginger root first, then add the mushrooms, gizzard, ham, shrimps and bamboo shoots. Stir a few times, then add the salt, soy sauce and wine or sherry. Stir constantly until well blended, then turn off the heat, add the cooked rice and mix all the ingredients together well to form the stuffing.
5. Pack the stuffing into the duck cavity and close up the tail opening. Place the duck on a wire tray on the top of a baking tin and put in a preheated oven for 30 minutes, then reduce the heat for a further 45 minutes.
6. Place the cooked duck on a serving dish, scrape out the stuffing and serve it in a separate bowl. Either carve the duck at the table or cut it into small pieces and garnish with finely chopped spring onions.

Eight-treasure duck; Steamed chicken with mushrooms

酒蒸鸡

DRUNKEN CHICKEN

1 × 1¼ kg (2½-2¾ lb) young chicken
2½ teaspoons salt
150 ml (¼ pint) rice wine or dry sherry
25 ml (1 fl oz) brandy
2 slices ginger root, peeled
2-3 spring onions, cut into short lengths
freshly ground black pepper

Preparation time: 5-10 minutes
Cooking time: about 1 hour 40 minutes

No liquid whatever other than the rice wine or dry sherry and brandy are used in cooking this dish, so that it is highly aromatic. The chicken should be so tender that the meat can be torn off with chopsticks without any effort.

1. Blanch the chicken in a saucepan of boiling water for 1 minute, remove and rinse in cold water.
2. Place the chicken (breast side down) in a large bowl, add 1½ teaspoons of the salt, wine or sherry, brandy, ginger root and spring onions. Place the bowl in a steamer and steam vigorously for 1½ hours. Remove and place the chicken on a serving dish (breast side up).
3. Pour about half the cooking liquid into a saucepan, add the remaining salt and some pepper to taste, bring to the boil, then pour it over the chicken and serve.

清炖狮子頭

YANGCHOW 'LION'S HEAD' (PORK MEATBALLS WITH CHINESE CABBAGE)

500 g (1¼ lb) pork, not too lean
2 slices ginger root, peeled and finely chopped
2 spring onions, finely chopped
2 teaspoons salt
2 tablespoons rice wine or dry sherry
1 tablespoon cornflour
1 Chinese cabbage
2 tablespoons oil
300 ml (½ pint) Stock (page 28)

Preparation time: 20-25 minutes
Cooking time: about 50 minutes

This famous dish originated from Yangchow in the Yangtse River delta: the pork meatballs are supposed to resemble the shape of a lion's head and the cabbage to look like its mane, hence the name.

1. Finely mince or chop the pork, mix with the ginger root, spring onions, salt, wine or sherry and cornflour. Shape the mixture into 4-6 meatballs.
2. Cut the cabbage into large chunks. Heat the oil in a saucepan, then stir-fry the cabbage for about 1 minute. Place the meatballs on top and add the stock, bring to the boil, then cover and simmer gently for 45 minutes. Serve hot.

Variation:
You can use 2 tablespoons soy sauce and 1 tablespoon sugar when making the meatballs – but remember to reduce the amount of salt to ½ teaspoon. The meat will have a darker and richer appearance.

五香排骨
FIVE-SPICE PORK SPARE-RIBS

750 g (1½-1¾ lb) pork spare ribs
1 teaspoon salt
1 tablespoon sugar
2 tablespoons rice wine or dry sherry
2 tablespoons soy sauce
1 teaspoon five-spice powder
1 tablespoon Hoi Sin or barbecue sauce

Preparation time: 10-15 minutes, plus marinating
Cooking time: 40-45 minutes for roasting or
**   10-15 minutes for grilling**
Oven: 200°C, 400°F, Gas Mark 6

1. First cut the meat into individual ribs; then, if you have a cleaver, chop each rib into 2 or 3 small pieces (if not, ask your butcher to prepare the meat). In a shallow, ovenproof dish, mix the pieces in the salt, sugar, wine or sherry, soy sauce, five-spice powder and Hoi Sin or barbecue sauce, then leave to marinate for at least 1 hour, turning over once or twice.
2. Cook the ribs in a preheated oven for 40-45 minutes, turning them once.
3. Alternatively, they can be barbecued on an open grill for about 10-15 minutes, turning them once or twice, until brown all over.

Variation:
The Hoi Sin or barbecue sauce can be replaced with 1 teaspoon chilli sauce, 1 teaspoon vinegar mixed with 2 teaspoons cornflour and one crushed clove of garlic.

豉汁蒸排骨
CANTONESE STEAMED PORK SPARE RIBS IN BLACK BEAN SAUCE

450 g (1 lb) pork spare ribs
1 clove garlic, crushed and finely chopped
1 slice ginger root, peeled and finely chopped
1 tablespoon black bean sauce
1 tablespoon soy sauce
1 tablespoon rice wine or dry sherry
1 teaspoon sugar
1 teaspoon cornflour
To garnish:
2 spring onions, cut into short lengths
1 small red pepper or chilli, thinly shredded
1 teaspoon sesame seed oil

Preparation time: about 15 minutes, plus marinating
Cooking time: 25-30 minutes

1. Chop the spare ribs into small pieces, mix with the garlic, ginger root, black bean sauce, soy sauce, wine or sherry, sugar and cornflour, then marinate for 15-20 minutes.
2. Place the spare ribs on a heatproof plate, put in a steamer and steam vigorously for 25-30 minutes. Garnish with spring onions, red chilli or pepper and sesame seed oil. Serve hot.

LEFT TO RIGHT: Yangchow 'Lion's head'; Five-spice pork spare-ribs

清蒸鱸魚

CANTONESE STEAMED SEA BASS

1 × 500 g (1¼ lb) sea bass or trout
1 teaspoon salt
1 teaspoon sesame seed oil
4 spring onions
3 Chinese dried mushrooms, soaked and thinly shredded
50 g (2 oz) pork fillet, thinly shredded
2 tablespoons light soy sauce
1 tablespoon rice wine or dry sherry
2 teaspoons cornflour
2 slices ginger root, peeled and thinly shredded
2 tablespoons oil

Preparation time: about 25 minutes
Cooking time: 15-20 minutes

1. Scale and clean the sea bass. Dry thoroughly, then slash both sides of the fish diagonally as deep as the bone at intervals of about 2 cm (¾ inch). Rub half the salt and all the sesame seed oil inside the fish and place it on top of 2-3 spring onions on a heatproof dish.
2. Mix the mushrooms and pork with the remaining salt, 1 tablespoon of the soy sauce, the wine or sherry and cornflour. Stuff half of this mixture inside the fish and the rest on top, with the ginger root. Place in a steamer and steam vigorously for 15 minutes.
3. Meanwhile, cut the remaining spring onions into short lengths and heat the oil in a pan until bubbling.
4. Remove the fish dish from the steamer. Pour off about half of the cooking liquid, then arrange the cut spring onions on top. Pour over the remaining soy sauce and then the hot oil. Serve hot.

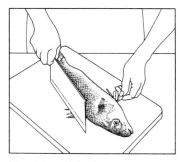
First trim off the fins.

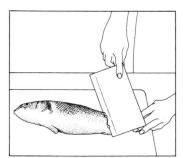
Remove scales from tail to head.

Clean, then pat the fish dry.

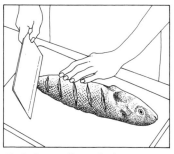
Slash diagonally to the bone.

糖醋全魚

SWEET AND SOUR WHOLE FISH

1 × 750 g (1½ lb) sea bass or grey mullet
1 teaspoon salt
½ teaspoon freshly ground white pepper
2 tablespoons rice wine or dry sherry
oil for deep frying
2 tablespoons cornflour
2 spring onions, finely chopped
2 slices ginger root, peeled and finely chopped
2 tablespoons sugar
2 tablespoons vinegar
2 tablespoons Stock (page 28) or water
½ teaspoon dark soy sauce
1 teaspoon sesame seed oil

Preparation time: about 15 minutes, plus marinating
Cooking time: 15-20 minutes

1. Scale and clean the fish, slash both sides of the skin diagonally as far as the bone at intervals of 1 cm (½ inch). Rub with the salt and pepper both inside and out, then leave to marinate in wine or sherry for 30 minutes to 1 hour.
2. Heat the oil in a wok or deep saucepan, coat the fish with about 1½ tablespoons of the cornflour and deep-fry it over a high heat for 3 minutes. Reduce the heat to low and fry for a further 3 minutes, then increase the heat to high again and continue frying the fish until golden brown all over. Remove the fish and place on a serving dish.
3. Pour off most of the oil, leaving about 1 tablespoon in the wok or pan. Put in the spring onions, ginger root, sugar and vinegar, then the remaining cornflour mixed with the stock or water and the soy sauce, stirring constantly to make a smooth sauce. Add the sesame seed oil and pour the sauce over the fish. Serve hot.

In China, a fish weighing less than 1 kg (2 lb) is often cooked whole, the ideal size would be a 500-750 g (1¼-1½ lb) sea bass or trout.

The fish is slashed on both sides to prevent the skin from bursting when cooking in hot oil, to allow the heat to penetrate quickly and at the same time to help diffuse the flavour of the seasonings.

Always choose a fresh fish. The usual rules are that its eyes should be clear and full, not sunken; that its gills should be bright red; that the body should be firm, not flabby; and finally that it should smell pleasantly fresh.

CLOCKWISE FROM THE RIGHT: Cantonese steamed trout; Red mullet in black bean sauce; Sweet and sour whole fish

豉汁燒紅鯔魚

RED MULLET IN BLACK BEAN SAUCE

1 × 450 g (1 lb) red mullet or snapper
1 teaspoon salt
1 tablespoon cornflour
4 tablespoons oil
1 clove garlic, crushed
2 slices ginger root, peeled and thinly shredded
1 small green pepper, cored, seeded and sliced
2 tablespoons salted black beans, crushed
2 tablespoons rice wine or dry sherry

Preparation time: 15 minutes
Cooking time: 15-20 minutes

1. Scale and clean the fish. Slash both sides of the fish diagonally as far as the bone at intervals of 2 cm (¾ inch). Dry thoroughly, then rub with the salt both inside and out, then coat with the cornflour.
2. Heat about half the oil in a wok or frying pan and stir-fry the garlic, ginger root and green pepper. Add the crushed black beans, blend well, then remove with a perforated spoon.
3. Heat the remaining oil in the wok or pan and fry the fish on both sides for 2-3 minutes. Return the green pepper and black bean mixture to the wok or pan, together with the wine or sherry. Cook for 2-3 minutes, carefully turning the fish once.
4. Place the fish on a serving dish and arrange the green pepper mixture on top. Serve hot.

干烧鱼

SICHUAN BRAISED FISH IN CHILLI SAUCE

1 × 750 g (1½ lb) fish (sea bass, carp, grey mullet or trout)
oil for deep frying
2 slices ginger root, peeled and finely chopped
1 clove garlic, crushed and finely chopped
2 tablespoons chilli bean paste
1 tablespoon soy sauce
2 tablespoons rice wine or dry sherry
½ teaspoon salt
3 tablespoons Stock (page 28)
1 teaspoon sugar
2 teaspoons vinegar
1 teaspoon chilli sauce
2 teaspoons cornflour mixed with 1 tablespoon water
2 spring onions, finely chopped, to garnish

Preparation time: about 15 minutes
Cooking time: 10-15 minutes

The amount of chilli bean paste and chilli sauce can either be increased or reduced according to how hot you like your food. If you have difficulty in finding chilli bean paste, substitute with crushed yellow bean sauce mixed with chilli sauce.

1. Scale and clean the fish. Slash both sides of the fish diagonally as deep as the bone at intervals of about 2 cm (¾ inch).
2. Heat the oil in a wok or deep saucepan until hot and deep fry the fish for about 5 minutes, turning it over once. Remove the fish.
3. Pour off most of the oil, leaving about 1 tablespoon in the wok or pan, add the ginger root, garlic, chilli bean paste, soy sauce and wine or sherry, stirring until smooth, then return the fish to the wok or pan, together with the salt and stock. Reduce the heat and simmer for 2-3 minutes, then turn the fish over, and add the sugar, vinegar, chilli sauce and cornflour and water paste. Increase heat to high to thicken the sauce. Garnish with finely chopped spring onions and serve hot.

> The Chinese casserole known as the sand-pot is made of clay with a coarse, sandy-textured beige exterior (often encased in a network of wire) and a dark brown, smoothly glazed interior.
> *Never* place an empty sand-pot on the heat; there should always be liquid in the pot to prevent it from cracking. *Never* place a hot casserole on damp or cold surface until it has cooled; the combination of hot pot and wet or cold surface will crack the pot.

豆腐烧鱼

FISH AND BEAN CURD CASSEROLE

450 g (1 lb) fish steak (cod, haddock or salmon)
1½ tablespoons flour
3-4 Chinese dried mushrooms
2 cakes bean curd
2 spring onions
2 slices ginger root, peeled
oil for deep frying
1 teaspoon salt
1 teaspoon sugar
1 tablespoon soy sauce
2 tablespoons rice wine or dry sherry
300 ml (½ pint) Stock (page 28)
fresh coriander leaves or parsley sprigs, to garnish
  (optional)

Preparation time: 20-25 minutes
Cooking time: 25-30 minutes

You can use more than one type of fish for this dish; the less expensive salmon heads and tails, which are sometimes available, are ideal.

1. Cut the fish into about 6 pieces and coat them with the flour.
2. Soak the mushrooms in warm water for 20 minutes, squeeze dry, discard the hard stalks and, depending on their size, cut them in half or quarters.
3. Cut each bean curd into about 8 pieces and cut the spring onions and ginger root into short lengths.
4. Heat the oil in a wok or deep fryer and fry the fish pieces over a moderate heat for 5 minutes or until golden. Remove and drain.
5. In the same oil, fry the bean curd pieces until golden. Remove and drain.
6. Place the bean curd, fish pieces and mushrooms in a casserole or a Chinese sand-pot (or saucepan). Add the salt, sugar, soy sauce, wine or sherry, spring onions, ginger root and the stock. Bring to the boil, then reduce the heat, cover and simmer for 10 minutes. Garnish with fresh coriander or parsley (if using) and serve in the casserole.

Chinese cabbage casserole; Sichuan braised fish in chilli sauce

沙鍋白菜

CHINESE CABBAGE CASSEROLE

750 g (1½-1¾ lb) Chinese cabbage
3-4 Chinese dried mushrooms
1 tablespoon dried shrimps
450 g (1 lb) bamboo shoots or carrots
50 g (2 oz) cooked ham
300 ml (½ pint) Stock (page 28)
1 teaspoon salt
1 tablespoon rice wine or dry sherry

Preparation time: 15-20 minutes
Cooking time: about 35 minutes

1. Discard the tough, outer cabbage leaves, trim off the hard root, then cut the cabbage into 3-4 sections depending on its length. Place the sections on the bottom of a casserole or Chinese sand-pot (or saucepan).
2. Soak the dried mushrooms and shrimps in hot water for 10 minutes. Squeeze dry the mushrooms, reserving the water. Discard the hard stalks, then place them and the shrimps on top of the cabbage sections.
3. Cut the bamboo shoots or carrots into thin slices and place them on top.
4. Cut the ham into thin slices also and add to the pot.
5. Finally add the stock together with the reserved water to the pot. The level of liquid should be not too near the top as a lot of water will come out of the cabbage during cooking. Now add the salt and cook gently for 30 minutes over a moderate heat.
6. Just before serving, add the wine or sherry, bring to the boil and serve hot.

紅扒鵪鶉蛋

BRAISED QUAIL'S EGGS WITH MUSHROOMS

24 quail's eggs
2 tablespoons soy sauce
2 tablespoons cornflour
225 g (8 oz) mange-tout peas, broccoli or asparagus
1-2 carrots, peeled
1 teaspoon salt
1 teaspoon sugar
1 teaspoon sesame seed oil
300 ml (½ pint) Stock (page 28)
oil for deep frying
1 × 425 g (15 oz) can of straw mushrooms, drained or 225 g (8 oz) fresh button mushrooms

Preparation time: about 25 minutes
Cooking time: about 1 hour

If fresh quail's eggs are unavailable, use a 425 g (15 oz) can. It contains about 30 quail's eggs already cooked and shelled. Just drain off the water and omit the steaming and shelling process.

1. Put the quail's eggs in a bowl, cover with cold water, place in a steamer and steam vigorously for 10 minutes. Remove the eggs and plunge them into cold water for 5 minutes, then shell them and marinate in the soy sauce for about 20 minutes, turning them frequently. Remove the eggs and coat each one with 1 tablespoon of the cornflour, reserving the marinade.
2. Wash, top and tail the mange-touts, or cut the broccoli or asparagus into 5-7.5 cm (2-3 inch) lengths. Cut the carrots into roughly the same size.
3. Mix the salt, sugar, sesame seed oil, the remaining cornflour and the stock together with the marinade.
4. Heat the oil in a wok or deep saucepan until hot, then deep fry the eggs until golden. Remove and drain.
5. Pour off most of the oil, leaving about 2 tablespoons in the wok or pan, then stir-fry the mange-touts, broccoli or asparagus and the carrots with about ⅓ of the sauce mixture for 1½-2 minutes. Remove and arrange neatly around the edge of a serving dish.
6. Heat up about 2 more tablespoons of the oil until hot, then stir-fry the mushrooms for about 30 seconds. Add the eggs with the remaining sauce, mix thoroughly and when the sauce is smooth and beginning to thicken, pour together with the eggs and mushrooms on to the middle of the vegetables. Serve hot.

TOP TO BOTTOM: Cantonese crab cooked in black bean sauce; Bean curd with assorted meats; Braised quail's eggs with mushrooms

什錦豆腐

BEAN CURD WITH ASSORTED MEATS

2 cakes bean curd
50 g (2 oz) cooked ham
100 g (4 oz) fresh mushrooms
100 g (4 oz) bamboo-shoots
100 g (4 oz) cooked meat (pork, beef or lamb)
300 ml (½ pint) Stock (page 28)
1 teaspoon salt
1 tablespoon soy sauce
225 g (8 oz) broccoli or lettuce heart
100 g (4 oz) peeled prawns
2 tablespoons oil

Preparation time: 20-25 minutes
Cooking time: 1¼ hours

Any leftover meat from a roasted joint is perfect for this dish.

1. Cut the bean curd into about 20 small cubes. Dice the ham, mushrooms, bamboo-shoots and cooked meat also into small cubes.
2. Place all the ingredients into a casserole or Chinese sand-pot (or saucepan). Add the stock, salt and soy sauce, gently bring it to the boil and cook uncovered over a low heat for 1 hour.
3. Just before serving, stir-fry the broccoli or lettuce heart and peeled prawns in hot oil for 1½-2 minutes, then place them on top of the casserole and serve. If you have used a saucepan instead of a casserole, then transfer the entire contents into a serving bowl first, then place the stir-fried greens and prawns on top.

Fresh bean-curd sealed in a small container and packaged under the name *tofu* is the Japanese variety. It is extremely soft and silky but does not absorb other flavours as readily as the firmer Chinese sort. Also it tends to fall apart in stir-frying, therefore it is not suitable for Chinese cooking, except for soup recipes. Blanching bean-curd for 2-3 minutes will harden the texture, so that it will not fall apart so easily when stir-frying.

Freezing bean-curd will give it a beehive-like and slightly tough texture, it is then more suitable for the slow, long-cooking methods.

豉椒焗螃蟹

CANTONESE CRAB COOKED IN BLACK BEAN SAUCE

2 × 450-500 g (1-1¼ lb) crabs
1 tablespoon soy sauce
2 tablespoons rice wine or dry sherry
1 tablespoon cornflour
3 tablespoons oil
1 clove garlic, crushed and finely chopped
4 slices ginger root, peeled and finely chopped
2-3 spring onions, finely chopped
2 tablespoons crushed black bean sauce
1 tablespoon vinegar
2-3 tablespoons Stock (page 28) or water

Preparation time: about 20-25 minutes
Cooking time: about 10 minutes

This dish is best eaten with your fingers. You can have a bowl of warm water with a segment or two of lemon in it to act as a finger bowl.

1. Wash the shells and break each crab into 3 or 4 pieces, separating the legs and claws. Crack the shells. Discard the feathery gills and the sac.
2. Marinate the crab pieces in the soy sauce, wine or sherry and cornflour for 10 minutes.
3. Heat the oil in a preheated wok or frying-pan, put in the garlic, ginger root and spring onions to flavour the oil, then add the crushed black bean sauce, stirring until smooth. Put in the crab, stirring constantly for 1½-2 minutes, then add the vinegar and stock or water. Continue stirring until thickened. Serve hot.

Separate the legs and claws.

Crack the claws with the back of the cleaver.

Crack the shell into 2-3 pieces.

Discard the feathery gills and sac.

什錦火鍋

CHINESE HOT-POT

450 g (1 lb) lamb fillet (or pork, beef or all three)
225 g (8 oz) chicken breast, boned and skinned
225 g (8 oz) peeled prawns (or fish fillet or both)
225 g (8 oz) fresh mushrooms
450 g (1 lb) Chinese cabbage (or spinach)
2-3 cakes bean curd
225 g (8 oz) transparent (cellophane) noodles or 450 g (1 lb)
   egg noodles
1¾ litres (3 pints) Stock (page 28) or water
Dip sauce:
6 tablespoons soy sauce
2 teaspoons sugar
1 teaspoon sesame seed oil
3-4 spring onions, finely chopped
3 slices ginger root, peeled and finely chopped

Preparation time: 35-40 minutes

A Chinese hot-pot is like a fondue, when the actual cooking is done not in the kitchen but on the dining table by each individual. Also known as Mongolian fire-pot, the Chinese hot-pot has a funnel at the centre in which charcoal is burned. The moat is filled with stock or water and you cook your own food in the boiling liquid, then dip it in the sauce before eating it.

1. Cut the meat and chicken into slices as thin as you possibly can; arrange them either separately on a large plate or together in small individual dishes.
2. Cut the prawns or fish into small slices also. Thinly slice the mushrooms and cut the cabbage or spinach and bean curd all into small pieces.
3. Soak the noodles until soft and arrange everything neatly, either together or separately like the meats.
4. Mix all the ingredients for the dip sauce together and pour into 4-6 little dishes. Place them on the table within easy reach of everyone.
5. Bring the stock or water to a fast boil, then each person picks up a piece of meat of his or her choice with chopsticks (or a fork) and dips it into the boiling liquid for a short time – usually as soon as the colour of the meat changes, it is done – then quickly retrieves it, dips it into the sauce and eats it while piping hot.
6. When all the meats have been eaten, add all the vegetables to the pot, boil vigorously for a few minutes, then ladle out the contents into individual bowls, add the remaining dip sauce and serve as a most delicious soup to finish off the meal.

RICE, NOODLES & PANCAKES

什錦炒面

CHOW MEIN (FRIED NOODLES WITH ASSORTED MEATS)

Serves 6-8 on its own
Serves 10-12 as part of a cold buffet
100 g (4 oz) pork fillet
100 g (4 oz) cooked ham
100 g (4 oz) peeled prawns
100 g (4 oz) carrots
100 g (4 oz) fresh bean sprouts
100 g (4 oz) mange-touts peas or French beans
2-3 spring onions
2-3 eggs
1½ teaspoons salt
4 tablespoons oil
450 g (1 lb) fresh or dried Chinese egg noodles
1 teaspoon sugar
2½ tablespoons soy sauce
1 tablespoon rice wine or dry sherry

Preparation time: 20-25 minutes

1. Thinly shred the pork and ham. If using king prawns, cut each one into 2-3 pieces, smaller prawns can be left whole.
2. Thinly shred the carrots. Wash the bean sprouts and mange-tout peas or top and tail the French beans. Cut the spring onions into short lengths.
3. Beat the eggs with a pinch of the salt. Heat 1 tablespoon of the oil in a preheated wok or frying pan and pour in the beaten eggs evenly to make a large, thin egg 'pancake'. Turn it over carefully to cook both sides, then remove to a chopping board and let it cool a little before cutting it into thin strips.
4. Bring a saucepan of water to the boil, add the noodles and separate them with a pair of chopsticks or a fork. Bring back to the boil and add 1 cup of cold water. Bring back to the boil once more and stir to separate, then, when the noodles start to float to the top, drain in a sieve and rinse with cold water.
5. Heat up the remaining oil, stir-fry the spring onions, pork, ham, prawns, carrots, bean sprouts and mange-tout peas or French beans with the remaining salt, the sugar and wine or sherry, stirring over a high heat for about 1 minute, then add the noodles and egg strips with the soy sauce. Continue stirring until all the ingredients are well blended. Serve either hot or cold.

湯面

NOODLES IN SOUP

225 g (8 oz) chicken breast, boned and skinned (or pork or lamb fillet)
1½ teaspoons salt
2 teaspoons cornflour
100 g (4 oz) fresh mushrooms
100 g (4 oz) bamboo shoots
½ cucumber
2-3 spring onions
2 slices ginger root, peeled
350 g (12 oz) fresh or dried Chinese egg noodles
600 ml (1 pint) Stock (page 28)
3 tablespoons oil
3 tablespoons light soy sauce
1 tablespoon rice wine or dry sherry
2 teaspoons sesame seed oil (optional), to garnish

Preparation time: about 15-20 minutes

1. Cut the chicken breast or meat into matchstick-sized shreds and mix with ½ teaspoon of the salt and the cornflour.
2. Thinly shred the mushrooms, bamboo shoots and cucumber. Cut the spring onions and ginger root into thin shreds also.
3. Cook the noodles as described in the recipe for *Chow Mein* (opposite). Drain, do not rinse in cold water but place them in either a large serving bowl or in 4 individual bowls.
4. Bring the stock to the boil and pour over the cooked noodles.
5. Heat the oil in a preheated wok or frying pan and add the spring onions and ginger root followed by the chicken or meat, mushrooms, bamboo shoots and cucumber. Stir a few times, then add the remaining salt, 2 tablespoons of the soy sauce and wine or sherry. Cook for about 1-1½ minutes, stirring constantly. Pour the mixture over the noodles, garnish with the remaining soy sauce and sesame seed oil (if using). Serve hot.

TOP TO BOTTOM: Chow mein; Noodles in soup

什錦燴飯（廣東式）

CANTONESE RICE

225 g (8 oz) rice
350 ml (12 fl oz) water
100 g (4 oz) squid or prawns
8 ready made fish balls or 100 g (4 oz) fish fillet
1 pork kidney
1 chicken liver
100 g (4 oz) roast pork or any type of meat
100 g (4 oz) seasonal greens (broccoli, mange-touts, French
    beans or cabbage)
2 spring onions
3 tablespoons oil
1 teaspoon salt
1 teaspoon sugar
2 tablespoons soy sauce
2 teaspoons cornflour
4 tablespoons Stock (page 28)
2 teaspoons sesame seed oil (optional)

Preparation time: 30 minutes

This is a very popular dish served in Cantonese
restaurants, known as *Mixed meats* or *Assorted meats
with rice*. The ingredients vary enormously according
to the chef's whims or seasonal availabilities. This
recipe is only a suggestion, you may add or substitute
as you like, or use any convenient leftovers.

1. Cook the rice in the water as described in the recipe
for *Plain boiled rice* (page 79) and keep hot.
2. Prepare the squid as described in the recipe for
Stir-fried squid flowers (page 50), or if using prawns,
prepare them as described in the recipe for *Red and
white prawns with green vegetable* (page 46), using egg
white and cornflour in the same way.
3. If using fish fillets instead of fish balls, cut it to the
same size as the fish in *Fish Slices with wine sauce*
(page 49).
4. Prepare the kidney as described in the recipe for
Stir-fried kidney-flowers Shandong style (page 43).
5. Cut the chicken liver and meat into small slices.
6. Wash and cut the greens into small slices also; and
cut the spring onions into short lengths.
7. Blanch the squid or prawns, kidney, liver and
greens in boiling water for 10-15 seconds, remove and
drain.
8. Heat the oil in a preheated wok or frying pan and
put in the spring onions, followed by all the meat, fish
and vegetables. Add the salt, sugar and soy sauce, stir a
few times, then add the cornflour mixed with the
stock. Continue stirring, until everything is well
blended, then add the sesame seed oil. Serve hot on
top of a bed of cooked rice on 4 individual plates.

什錦炒飯

YANGCHOW FRIED RICE

3-4 Chinese dried mushrooms or 50 g (2 oz) fresh button
   mushrooms
50 g (2 oz) bamboo shoots or carrots
50 g (2 oz) green peas or 1 small green pepper, cored and
   seeded
100 g (4 oz) peeled prawns
100 g (4 oz) cooked ham or pork
2-3 eggs
1 teaspoon salt
2 spring onions, finely chopped
3 tablespoons oil
350 g-450 g (12 oz-1 lb) cooked rice or 175 g-225 g (6-8 oz)
   raw rice, cooked as *Plain boiled rice* (page 79)
1½ tablespoons light soy sauce

Preparation time: 25 minutes

This very popular dish must have originated from the
river port Yangchow on the Yangtse Delta, but it is
now on the menu of almost every Cantonese res-
taurant. As you can see from the list of ingredients, you
can substitute or vary them as you wish. Ideally use
cooked rice that is cold and hard; if you have to cook
some rice specially for this dish, then cook it well in
advance and leave it to cool.

1. If using dried mushrooms soak them in warm water
for 20 minutes, squeeze dry and discard the hard
stalks, then dice into small cubes the size of the peas. If
using button mushrooms, leave small ones whole, cut
large ones to the same size as the peas. Cut the bamboo
shoots or carrots and the green pepper (if using) into
same-sized cubes. The prawns can be left whole if
small, otherwise cut each one into 2-3 pieces. Dice the
ham or pork into small cubes also.
2. Lightly beat the eggs with a pinch of the salt and
about half the spring onions.
3. Heat about 1 tablespoon of the oil in a preheated
wok or frying pan, scramble the eggs, then remove.
4. Heat up the remaining oil, add all the vegetables
together with the prawns and ham or pork. Stir a few
times, then add the cooked rice with the remaining salt
and soy sauce, stirring to separate each grain of rice.
Finally add the scrambled eggs, breaking them into
small pieces. Add the remaining spring onions as a
garnish and serve hot.

炒米粉

FRIED RICE-NOODLES

450 g (1 lb) rice-noodles
1 tablespoon dried shrimps
100 g (4 oz) bamboo shoots
100 g (4 oz) pork
2 sticks celery
50 g (2 oz) leeks or spring onions
4 tablespoons oil
1 teaspoon salt
4 tablespoons Stock (page 28)
2 tablespoons light soy sauce

Preparation time: about 20 minutes

It has not been established who first started to make
noodles, the Chinese or the Italians, but certainly
noodles have been eaten in China for more than
2000 years.
Also known as rice sticks, rice-noodles are very popular in southern China, where they are interchangeable
with noodles made with wheat-flour in most recipes.

1. Soak the rice-noodles in warm water for 10-15
minutes or until soft. Soak the dried shrimps for 20
minutes. Cut the bamboo shoots, pork, celery and leeks
or spring onions into matchstick-sized shreds.
2. Heat 2 tablespoons of the oil in a preheated wok or
frying pan, stir fry the pork, bamboo shoots, shrimps,
celery and leeks or spring onions. Add the salt and
stock and cook for about 2 minutes. Remove and reserve.
3. Add the remaining oil, drain the rice-noodles and
add to the wok or pan, stirring to make sure that each
'stick' is covered with oil, then add soy sauce and all
the other ingredients. Stir constantly for 1½-2 minutes
or until there is no juice left at all.

Variation:

For *Singapore fried rice-noodles*: use a small onion
instead of celery and add 2 teaspoons curry powder
during the last stage of cooking.

Fresh egg noodles are available in Chinese food stores
and Italian delicatessens. If dried egg noodles are used,
the narrow type is preferable to the flat ones; also
spaghetti, or the finer spaghettini, can be substituted.

TOP TO BOTTOM: Fried rice-noodles; Yangchow fried rice;
Cantonese rice

薄 餅

THIN PANCAKES

450 g (1 lb) plain flour
300 ml (½ pint) boiling water
1 tablespoon oil

Preparation time: about 25-30 minutes

These pancakes are traditionally served with dishes such as *Aromatic and crispy duck* (page 58) or *Mu-shu pork* (page 41), but of course you can serve them with almost any dish of your choice. These pancakes can be made well in advance and be warmed up by steaming for 5 minutes just before serving. Any leftovers can be stored in the refrigerator for a few days or can be frozen for up to 6 months.

1. Sift the flour into a mixing bowl and very gently pour in the boiling water mixed with 1 teaspoon oil, stirring as you pour.
2. Knead the mixture into a firm dough, then divide it into 3 equal portions. Roll out each portion into a long 'sausage' on a lightly floured surface and cut each 'sausage' into 8-10 pieces. Using the palm of your hand, press each piece into a flat pancake. Brush one side of the pancake with a little oil and place another on top to form a 'sandwich', so that you end up with 12 'sandwiches'.
3. Using a rolling pin on a lightly floured surface, flatten each 'sandwich' into a 15 cm (6 inch) circle, rolling gently on both sides.
4. Place an ungreased frying pan over a high heat. When it is hot, reduce the heat to moderate and put one pancake 'sandwich' at a time into the pan, turning it over when it starts to puff up with air bubbles. Remove when little brown spots appear on the underside and very gently peel apart the 2 layers. Fold each pancake in half and keep under a damp cloth until serving.

Brush one side of the flattened pancake with a little oil. Place a second on top to form a sandwich.

Roll out each sandwich on a lightly floured surface, using a rolling pin. Roll gently on both sides to form a 15 cm (6 inch) circle.

葱 油 餅

PEKING ONION PANCAKES

450 g (1 lb) plain flour
250 ml (8 fl oz) boiling water
50 ml (2 fl oz) cold water
10-12 spring onions, coarsely chopped
2 teaspoons salt
100 g (4 oz) lard or shortening
4 tablespoons oil

Preparation time: about 1 hour

One large or 2 medium ordinary onions, coarsely chopped, may be used in place of the spring onions.

1. Sift the flour into a mixing bowl and gently pour in the boiling water. Stir for 5 minutes, then add the cold water and knead into a firm dough. Cover with a damp cloth and leave to stand for 20-25 minutes.
2. Roll out the dough on a lightly floured surface and divide it into 10-12 sections. Roll each section into a flat pancake about 20 cm (8 inches) in diameter. Sprinkle each pancake evenly with the onions, salt and lard or shortening. Fold up from the sides, then roll again to make a 5 mm (¼ inch) thick pancake.
4. Heat the oil in a preheated frying pan and shallow fry the pancakes one at a time over a medium heat for about 5-6 minutes, turning over once. They should be golden brown and crispy. Serve either on their own with a soup or with any of the light dishes.

春 捲 (上海式)

SHANGHAI SPRING ROLLS

Makes about 20

1 pack 20 ready-made frozen spring roll skins
225 g (8 oz) pork fillet
1 tablespoon soy sauce
1 tablespoon rice wine or dry sherry
2 teaspoons cornflour
5-6 Chinese dried mushrooms
100 g (4 oz) bamboo shoots
225 g (8 oz) young tender leeks or spring onions
oil for deep frying
1 teaspoon salt
1 teaspoon sugar
1 teaspoon plain flour mixed with 2 teaspoons water
flour, for dusting

Dip sauce:

2 tablespoons vinegar
2 slices ginger root, peeled and thinly shredded

Preparation time: 35-40 minutes

The main feature of *Shanghai spring rolls* is that they do not contain bean sprouts. They are also small which makes them ideal for a buffet-style meal or as cocktail snacks.

RIGHT TO LEFT: Shanghai spring rolls; Thin pancakes;
Peking onion pancakes

1. Take the spring roll skins out of the packet and make sure they are thoroughly defrosted. Cover with a damp cloth to prevent them from drying out.
2. To make the filling, cut the pork into thin shreds and marinate in the soy sauce, wine or sherry and cornflour.
3. Soak the dried mushrooms in warm water for 20 minutes, squeeze dry and discard the hard stalks, then thinly shred. Cut the bamboo shoots and leeks or spring onions also into thin shreds.
4. Heat about 3 tablespoons of the oil in a preheated wok or frying pan, stir-fry the pork shreds until their colour changes, then scoop out with a perforated spoon. In the same wok or pan, add the shredded mushrooms, bamboo shoots and leeks or spring onions. Stir a few times, then add the salt and sugar, together with the pork. Cook together for 1½-2 minutes, then remove and leave it to cool a little.
5. To make the spring rolls, take 1 tablespoon of the filling, shape it into a 7.5 cm (3 inch) long sausage and place it on the spring roll skin about a third of the way down, lift the lower flap over the filling and roll once, then fold both ends, roll once more. Brush the upper edge with the flour and water mixture and roll it into a neat package. Repeat until all the filling is used up. Lightly dust a tray with flour and place the spring rolls in rows with the flap sides down. These can be kept in the refrigerator for a day or they can be frozen for up to 3 months.
6. To cook, heat the remaining oil in a wok or deep fryer and deep fry the spring rolls 5-6 at a time for 3-4 minutes or until golden and crispy. Remove and drain on kitchen paper. Serve hot with the vinegar and ginger root dip.

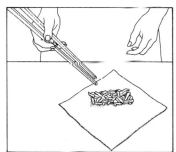
Place the filling on the spring roll skin.

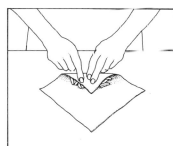
Roll over the lower flap.

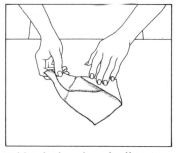
Fold in both ends and roll again.

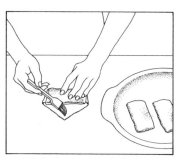
Brush the last corner before rolling up.

豆 沙 包

STEAMED DUMPLINGS WITH SWEET FILLINGS

2 teaspoons sugar
2 teaspoons dried yeast
300 ml (½ pint) warm water
450 g (1 lb) self-raising flour
1 × 510 g (1 lb 2 oz) can red bean paste

Preparation time: 2-2½ hours, plus rising
Cooking time: about 20 minutes

1. Dissolve the sugar and yeast in the warm water until frothy, 5-10 minutes. Sift the flour into a mixing bowl, then gradually stir in the yeast mixture to make a firm dough. Knead for 5 minutes, then cover with a damp cloth and leave in a warm place to rise for 1-1½ hours.
2. Knead the dough on a lightly floured surface for about 5 minutes, then roll into a long 'sausage'. Cut it into about 24 pieces and flatten each piece with the palm of your hand, then roll out each piece with a rolling pin into a pancake about 10 cm (4 inches) in diameter.
3. Place 1 tablespoon of the red bean paste in the centre of each pancake, then gather up the dough around the filling to meet at the top. Twist it to enclose the filling tightly. Leave to stand for at least 20 minutes before cooking.
4. Place a piece of wet muslin on the rack of a steamer, arrange the dumplings 2.5 cm (1 inch) apart on the muslin, cover and steam vigorously for 20 minutes. Serve hot.

Roll the dough into a sausage.

Cut and flatten each piece.

Place the filling in the centre.

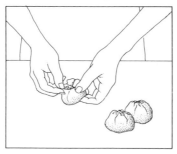
Draw up and twist to enclose.

小 笼 肉 包

STEAMED DUMPLINGS WITH SAVOURY FILLINGS

Makes 30-35
450 g (1 lb) plain flour
300 ml (½ pint) water
Filling:
450 g (1 lb) pork (or lamb or beef)
225 g (8 oz) bamboo shoots
3-4 spring onions, finely chopped
3 slices ginger root, peeled and finely chopped
1 teaspoon salt
2 teaspoons sugar
2 tablespoons light soy sauce
2 tablespoons rice wine or dry sherry
2 tablespoons Stock (page 28)
1 teaspoon sesame seed oil
1 small cabbage, separated into leaves
Dip sauce:
2 tablespoons soy sauce mixed with 1 tablespoon vinegar

Preparation time: 1½-2 hours
Cooking time: about 20 minutes

Ready minced meat can be used but the texture will be slightly less interesting.

1. Sift the flour into a mixing bowl, pour in the water and mix to a stiff dough. Knead for 5 minutes, then leave the dough in the bowl covered with a damp cloth, for 10 minutes.
2. To make the filling, coarsely chop the meat and bamboo shoots, add the spring onions, ginger root, salt, sugar, soy sauce, wine or sherry, stock and sesame seed oil. Mix and blend thoroughly.
3. Roll out the dough into 2 long 'sausages' on a lightly floured surface. Cut each 'sausage' into 16-18 pieces. Flatten each piece with the palm of your hand, then use a rolling pin to roll out each piece into a pancake about 7.5 cm (3 inches) in diameter.
4. Place 1 tablespoon of the filling in the centre of each pancake, fold the pancake firmly over the filling, press and roll the edges tightly together to close at the top.
5. Line the rack of a steamer with the cabbage leaves, place the dumplings on the cabbage, cover and steam vigorously for 20 minutes. Serve with the soy sauce and vinegar dip. Any leftovers can be reheated either by steaming for 5 minutes or shallow-frying in a little oil for 5-6 minutes.

CLOCKWISE FROM THE TOP: Steamed dumplings with sweet fillings; Plain boiled rice; Steamed dumplings with savoury fillings

白 飯

PLAIN BOILED RICE

350 g (12 oz) long grain rice
450 ml (¾ pint) water

Preparation time: 5 minutes

This recipe uses 2 measures of rice to 3 of water. Should you prefer your rice to be softer and less fluffy, then use rounded, pudding rice and reduce the amount of water by a quarter.

1. Wash and rinse the rice in cold water.
2. Put the washed rice with the 450 ml (¾ pint) water in a saucepan. Bring it to the boil, then use a spoon to give it a stir in order to prevent the rice sticking to the bottom of the pan.
3. Reduce the heat to very low, cover and cook for 15 minutes. Turn off the heat and let the rice stand for 10 minutes or so. Then it is done.
4. Just before serving, fluff the rice up with a fork or spoon.

INDEX

Aromatic and crispy Sichuan duck 58
Aubergine with Sichuan 'fish sauce' 52

Bamboo shoots 9
Bean curd 9:
  Bean-curd with assorted meats 69
  Bean-curd soup 30
  Braised bean-curd 23
  Fish and bean-curd casserole 66
  Stir-fried spinach and bean-curd 53
Bean sprouts 9
Beef:
  Beef and green peppers in Cantonese black bean sauce 36
  Braised beef 54
  Cantonese beef in oyster sauce 37
  Sichuan dry-fried shredded beef 36
  Spiced beef 22
  Steamed beef Sichuan style 54
Braised broccoli 53

Cabbage:
  Hot and sour cabbage 22
  Sliced pork and cabbage soup 28
Cantonese beef in oyster sauce 37
Cantonese chicken, ham and greens 56
Cantonese crab cooked in black bean sauce 69
Cantonese rice 74
Cantonese soya braised chicken 18
Cantonese steamed pork spare ribs in black bean sauce 63
Cantonese steamed sea bass 64
Cantonese sweet and sour prawns 46
Celery:
  Chicken cubes with celery 44
  Shredded fish with celery 51
Cellophane or transparent noodles 9
Chicken:
  Cantonese chicken, ham and greens 56
  Cantonese soya braised chicken 18
  Chicken breast and egg white 44
  Chicken cubes with celery 44
  Chicken cubes with walnuts Sichuan style 38
  Chicken and ham soup 32
  Chicken wings assembly 57
  Diced chicken in Peking bean sauce 39
  Drunken chicken 61
  Jellied chicken 17
  Shanghai braised chicken 57
  Shredded chicken breast with green peppers 38
  Shredded chicken in mustard sauce 19
  Sichuan bang-bang chicken 19
  Steamed chicken with mushrooms 60
Chilli bean paste 9
Chilli sauce 9
Chinese cabbage casserole 67
Chinese cabbage, pork meatballs with 62
Chinese dried mushrooms 9
Chinese hot pot 70
Chinese mushroom soup 28
Chopsticks 11
Chow Mein 72
Crab:
  Cantonese crab cooked in black bean sauce 69
  Deep-fried crabmeat balls 47
Crispy 'seaweed' 24
Crystal-boiled pork with dip-sauce 22
Crystal-boiled prawns in jelly 17
Cucumber:
  Lamb and cucumber soup 32
  Sweet and sour cucumber 24

Deep-fried crabmeat balls 47
Dried shrimps 9
Drunken chicken 61
Drunken giblets 20
Duck:
  Aromatic and crispy Sichuan duck 58
  Eight-treasure duck 60
  Salted Peking duck 20
  Soya duck 19
Dumplings, steamed, with sweet or savoury fillings 78

Egg-drop soup 28
Eight-treasure duck 60
Eight-treasure soup 33

Fire-cooking 9
Fish:
  Braised fish steak 51
  Fish balls with vegetable soup 31
  Fish and bean-curd casserole 66
  Fish slices in hot sauce 17
  Fish slices with wine sauce 49
  Shanghai 'smoked' fish 16
  Shredded fish with celery 51
  Sichuan braised fish in chilli sauce 66
  Sliced fish soup 31
  Sweet and sour whole fish 64
Five-spice pork spare-ribs 63
Five-spice powder 9

Giblets:
  Drunken giblets 20
Ginger root 10

Hoi Sin sauce 10
Hors d'oeuvre 25-6
Hot-mixed prawns 14
Hot and sour cabbage 22

Jellied chicken 17

Kidney:
  Kidney salad 21
  Stir-fried kidney-flowers, Shandong style 43

Lamb:
  Lamb and cucumber soup 32
  Rapid-fried lamb slices 42
Liver:
  Fried liver Sichuan style 43
  Liver soup 30

Menu-making 11-13
Mu-Shu pork Shandong style 41
Mushroom:
  Braised quail's eggs with mushrooms 68
  Chinese dried mushrooms 9
  Chinese mushroom soup 28
  Steamed chicken with mushrooms 60

Noodles, fried, with assorted meats 72
Noodles in soup 72

Oil-cooking 9
Oyster sauce 10; Cantonese beef in 37

Pancakes:
  Peking onion pancakes 76
  Thin pancakes 76

Peking poached prawns 14
Phoenix-tail prawns 48
Pork:
  Cantonese steamed pork spare ribs in black bean sauce 63
  Crystal-boiled pork with dip-sauce 22
  Five-spice pork spare-ribs 63
  Mu-Shu pork Shandong style 41
  Pork with Sichuan preserved vegetable 41
  Pork slices with Chinese vegetables 34
  Pork spare ribs in Cantonese sweet and sour sauce 34
  Shanghai crispy meatballs 45
  Shanghai spring rolls 77
  Shredded pork in Peking bean sauce 44
  Sichuan fried pork spare ribs 40
  Spiced pork and cabbage soup 28
  Yangchow 'lion's head' 62
Prawn 10:
  Cantonese sweet and sour prawns 46
  Crystal-boiled prawns in jelly 17
  Hot-mixed prawns 14
  Peking poached prawns 14
  Phoenix-tail prawns 48
  Rapid-fried prawns in shells 14
  Red and white prawns with green vegetable 46
  Sichuan prawns in chilli and tomato sauce 51
Quail's eggs, braised, with mushrooms 68

Rapid-fried lamb slices 42
Rapid-fried prawns in shells 14
Red bean paste 10
Red mullet in black bean sauce 65
Red and white prawns with green vegetable 46
Rice:
  Cantonese rice 74
  Plain boiled rice 79
  Yangchow fried rice 75
Rice-noodles, fried 75

Salted black beans 10
Salted Peking duck 20
Sea bass:
  Cantonese steamed sea bass 64
  Sweet and sour whole fish 64
Sesame paste 10
Sesame seed oil 10
Shanghai braised chicken 57
Shanghai crispy meatballs 45
Shanghai 'smoked' fish 16
Shanghai spring rolls 77
Shredded chicken breast with green peppers 38
Shredded chicken in mustard sauce 19
Shredded fish with celery 51
Shredded pork in Peking bean sauce 44
Sichuan bang-bang chicken 19
Sichuan braised fish in chilli sauce 66
Sichuan dry-fried shredded beef 36
Sichuan fried pork spare ribs 40
Sichuan peppercorns 10
Sichuan preserved vegetable 10; pork with 41
Singapore fried rice-noodles 75
Sliced fish soup 31
Sliced pork and cabbage soup 28
Soy sauce 10
Soya duck 19
Spiced beef 22
Spinach, stir-fried, and bean-curd 53
Spring greens:
  Crispy 'seaweed' 24
Spring rolls 77

Squid flowers, stir-fried 50
Steam-cooking 9
Stock for soups 28
Sweet and sour cucumber 24
Sweet and sour whole fish 64
Sichuan prawns in chilli and tomato sauce 51

Three-flavours (pork, chicken and prawn) soup 32
Three sea-flavours (scallops, prawns and squid) 48
Tripe:
  Braised tripe 20

Vegetable:
  Fish balls with vegetable soup 31
  Pork slices with Chinese vegetables 34
  Red and white prawns with green vegetable 46
  Stir-fried mixed vegetables 53

Water chestnut 10
Water-cooking 9
Wok 10
Wooden ears 10

Yangchow fried rice 75
Yangchow 'lion's head' 62
Yellow bean sauce 10

LIST OF CHINESE AND ORIENTAL FOOD STORES

*will fill mail orders

Birmingham: Wing Yip Supermarket, 96 Coventry Street
Bournemouth: Sang Hing, 842 Christchurch Road, Boscombe
Bradford: Quality Foods, Southend Hall, Tickhill Street
Bristol: Wah Hing, 24 Lower Ashley Road, Montpelier
Canterbury: C&R Townsend, 24 Sun Street
Colchester: Golden Crown Oriental Supplies, 37 Crouch Street
Croydon: Lee Kiu, 230 High Street
Doncaster: Taisun, 49 College Road
Edinburgh: Loon Fung, 11 Howard Street
Glasgow: Chung Ying, 63 Cambridge Street
Hull: Sui Hing Co Ltd, 22 Story Street
Leeds: Wing Lee Hong, 6 Edward Street
Leicester: PKM Company, 5 Melton Street
Liverpool: Shun On, 27-35 Berry Street
London: *Cheong Leen, 4-10 Tower Street, WC2
*Ken Lo's Kitchen, 14 Eccleston Street, SW1
Manchester: Wing Yip Supermarket, 47a Faulkner Street
Newcastle-upon-Tyne: Wah Fung Hung, 87-9 Percy Street
Oxford: Palms Delicatessen, The Market
Plymouth: Wah Lung Supermarket, 95 Mayflower Street
Portsmouth: Eastern Stores, 214 Kingston Road
Romford: Eastyle, 11-12 Romford Shopping Hall, Market Place
Sheffield: Kung Heng Supermarket, 169 London Road
Southampton: Yau's Chinese Food Store, 9 St Mary Street